GEORGE WASHINGTON

~ The Writer ~

A Treasury of Letters, Diaries, and Public Documents

Compiled and Edited by Carolyn P. Yoder

Boyds Mills Press

To my parents
—C. P. Y.

ACKNOWLEDGMENTS

I would like to thank the following people for their help. Their insights and knowledge were extremely valuable and their patience much appreciated.

Dorothy Twohig, Editor-in-Chief Emeritus, Papers of George Washington, University of Virginia; Associate Professor Emeritus, University of Virginia

Lee Boyle, Historian, Valley Forge National Historical Park
Margaret Carlsen, Historian, Rockingham State Historic Site
Diane K. Depew, Colonial National Historical Park
Karie Diethorn, Chief Curator, Independence National Historical Park
Gordon Griffin, Former President, Rockingham State Historic Site
Karen A. Mason, Photographer
Mary Jane McFadden, Park Ranger, Fort Necessity National Battlefield
Montford H. R. Sayce, Professor Emeritus of Political Science, New England College

I would like to thank the following libraries, where I conducted a great deal of my research.
The David Library of the American Revolution
Franklin F. Moore Library, Rider University

Copyright © 2003 by Carolyn P. Yoder
All rights reserved

Boyds Mills Press, Inc.
A Highlights Company
815 Church Street
Honesdale, Pennsylvania 18431
Printed in China
Visit our Web site at
www.boydsmillspress.com

First edition, 2003
The text of this book is set in
12-point Goudy.

10 9 8 7 6 5 4 3 2 1

Publisher Cataloging in Publication Data

George Washington : the writer : a treasury of letters, diaries, and public documents / compiled and edited by Carolyn Yoder.
— 1st ed.
[144] p. : photos. ; cm.
Includes index.
Summary: A collection of letters, diary entries, speeches, and other documents written by George Washington, with brief introductions and archival photographs that provide historical background.
ISBN 1-56397-199-2
1. Washington, George, 1732–1799 — Correspondence.
2. Washington, George, 1732–1799 — Diaries.
I. Yoder, Carolyn. II. Title
973.41/ 092 B 21   2003
2002108915

COVER: *George Washington* (Munro-Lenox Portrait) by noted American portrait painter Gilbert Stuart, who lived from 1755 to 1828. Compare this portrait, painted after Washington's death, to the Lansdowne portrait on page 93. From the Collections of The New York Public Library, Astor, Lenox, and Tilden Foundations.

PAGE 3: Charles Willson Peale painted *George Washington at Princeton* in 1779, two years after the Battle of Princeton. Beyond the battlefield (behind Washington on left) appears the College of New Jersey (now Princeton University). The blue ribbon sash that Washington wears signifies that he is commander in chief.

CONTENTS

Editor's Note

The Papers of George Washington

George Washington by Gilbert Stuart

AT THE UNIVERSITY OF VIRGINIA IN CHARLOTTESVILLE, scholars are working to put together all the papers of Washington—papers written *by* him and *to* him—that are known to exist. It is considered the most complete collection of his correspondence and other writings ever assembled. The project, which is a joint effort between the University and the Mount Vernon Ladies' Association with the support of the National Endowment for the Humanities and the National Historical Publications and Records Commission, has been going on for more than thirty years and will most likely continue for at least another twenty. All in all, Washington's papers are expected to fill about ninety volumes.

The project is now at the halfway mark. The work is long, and attention is given to every word. The project's mission is to be totally faithful to the original papers. At present, all of Washington's diaries; a daybook kept during Washington's years as president; as well as the Colonial, the Confederation, and the Retirement Series, which are filled with letters, orders, and addresses, have been published. Work continues on the Revolutionary and the Presidential Series.

But in one sense the project's work is never done. It is always searching for more original Washington papers. Half of Washington's known original papers are at the Library of Congress. The others are in more than three hundred repositories in the United States, over seventy repositories overseas, and hundreds of private collections. Who knows where the next paper might be found?

Washington knew the value of his papers. He knew they would enhance his reputation and establish his legacy. During the Revolutionary War, he took extraordinary care of his papers, taking them with him from place to place as his headquarters moved. He even appointed a special secretary to oversee copying them. Washington knew that these papers would be a great source for the history of the Revolution.

In his later years, Washington worked on correcting his public papers—taking away, adding, or changing words.* When Washington returned to Mount Vernon in 1797, after his presidency, he thought about building a place to store his papers. That never happened. But Washington tried to make sure his papers would be taken care of after his death by bequeathing them to his nephew Bushrod.

Unfortunately, Bushrod Washington was not exactly the best person to handle Washington's papers. He allowed a good portion of them to leave Mount Vernon to be used by others. In the process, some of the papers were sold, given away, cut up, or lost by their custodians. Finally, in the 1800s, Washington's public and private papers were purchased by the U.S. government.

The work of the Charlottesville project is invaluable. The published series and diaries allowed me not only to put together this small anthology but also to get to know Washington as a young man, an officer, a farmer,

---

*The corrections appear mostly in Washington's papers written during the French and Indian War.

a family man, and as our country's first president. Washington's words made me understand and appreciate how he became larger than life while he lived and for many centuries later.

Some of the selections in this anthology are from John C. Fitzpatrick's The Writings of George Washington from the Original Manuscript Sources, 1745–1799, *which was published by authority of Congress in thirty-nine volumes, between 1931 and 1944.*

A NOTE ABOUT THE DIARIES

George Washington considered diary keeping as recording "where, how, or with whom my time is spent," with little space devoted to personal reflection. Washington wrote a daily record off and on in his late teens and twenties, but it wasn't until his mid-thirties that he became more serious and consistent in his record keeping. During most of the Revolutionary War, Washington was preoccupied with writing volumes of letters, orders, and addresses and did not have time to keep a diary. (From May to October in 1781, however, Washington recorded the entire Yorktown campaign, including the preparations made in New York and the march south.) After the war, Washington returned to diary keeping and remained faithful to it for the rest of his life. Unfortunately, few of the diaries from his presidential years survive. There are diaries on the trips to New England in 1789 and to the South in 1791 and on the Whiskey Rebellion in 1794. Most of the diaries that exist center on Washington's life at Mount Vernon. In documenting how he spent his time, Washington reveals a good deal about himself.

INTRODUCTION

MEET GEORGE WASHINGTON

This nineteenth-century engraving by John Rogers is based on a painting by Charles Willson Peale done in 1772, when Washington was forty. Standing in the wilderness where his military career began, Washington wears his uniform from the Virginia Regiment. He is pictured with a sword, gorget (decorative armor worn by officers), firearm, and orders in his pocket. The Peale portrait was the first time Washington posed for a painter.

ALTHOUGH GEORGE WASHINGTON NEVER WROTE his autobiography, his letters, speeches, and diaries tell us much about his life. Even the letters and addresses he wrote on the battlefields as a young man and as commander in chief are filled with his opinions, ideas, and desires. In letters to family and friends, Washington often mixed his views on military strategy with personal advice or affection. With Washington it is hard to separate the commander from the politician or the politician from the farmer. They tend to merge into one man.

Certainly not all of his major writings could be included here. Most of those that are here appear as excerpts. Washington often wrote long addresses and letters (except for talking face-to-face, writing was the only way to communicate at that time), and because he lived more than two centuries ago, his words are sometimes hard to recognize or follow. His style—and his poor spelling!—also get in the way.* The excerpts were carefully selected to show how he changed from year to year and how he handled those changes. The list of important dates that begins on page 119 puts his life into finer focus.

Little is known about Washington's life before the age of sixteen, when he started writing about it. Where he grew up and his family are about all we know. Almost nothing is known with certainty about Washington's schooling. Early biographers claim that Washington was tutored at home or was taught at a nearby school in Fredericksburg, Virginia, and that he studied mathematics, English, geography, handwriting, astronomy, and surveying.

After his father died, Washington's education and upbringing were slowly taken over by his half brother Lawrence, who groomed him for the life of a country gentleman. (Washington's formal education is said to have ended at the age of fifteen.) When Washington was fourteen, it was Lawrence who suggested a career in the navy, but Washington's mother decided against it. Instead, Washington took up surveying, a career that promised good money and plenty of adventure.

Washington was fiercely ambitious at a young age and set out to make a name for himself. He volunteered for a dangerous assignment in the wilderness, entered Virginia's military service (provincial troops under the command of Great Britain), and returned to the wilderness to fight in several campaigns. By the time he was twenty-one, people knew who Washington was. Two years later, he was called a hero.

At a young age, Washington paid close attention to reputation, honor, discipline, and the proper rules of conduct. He chose his bride—a rich widow—wisely. He carefully laid out and managed his fields, farms, and house at Mount Vernon. He invested in western lands. He held important political positions. He took life seriously. Every move was deliberate and every written word carefully thought out.

Later in life, honor for him became more closely associated with the greater good, the welfare of his country. Washington spoke out about England. He refused to buy British goods. He was a delegate to both

---

*According to John Fitzpatrick, "Washington, while no better a speller, was often no worse than his friends." He "spelled like a gentleman."

Continental Congresses. At the Second Continental Congress, he showed his devotion to the Patriot cause by attending many of the meetings in uniform. Unlike times in the past when he volunteered for military duty, Washington, now older and more mature, waited to be chosen as commander of the armed forces. He might have been sure of his appointment, but he didn't want to appear too bold. He had his reputation to think of. When it came time to select the president of the United States, Washington followed the same course. He didn't appear eager for the position but quietly waited until he was elected.

Throughout the Revolutionary War and his presidency, Washington's concern for his country and its cause was of utmost importance, overpowering his personal ambition and fame. He was passionate about independence, a strong and well-financed defense, and the need for a unified nation. He was intent on making sure that the country got off on the right footing, that it would become a leader among nations. During the times of his two retirements at Mount Vernon—after the war and after serving as president—he still was dedicated to this cause. At the age of sixty-six, he was even willing to reenter public life to fight the French, if needed, in order to keep the nation strong.

It is wrong to assume that Washington glided through life without worries, sadness, and defeats. Like everyone else, Washington was not immune from pain or disappointment. Some historians point to Washington's poor relationship with his mother as his biggest failure. And throughout his life, he was known for his temper. He tried to tame it, but it occasionally flared up. His letters show him at various times frustrated, jealous, angry, hurt, and scared. If nothing else, Washington was passionate.

Early in his life, Washington desperately wanted a commission in the British army, something he never got. He also constantly encountered money problems while running Mount Vernon and felt despair about the many slaves who worked and lived there. He survived the deaths of both his stepchildren and all of his brothers and sisters. He lost a number of battles during the Revolutionary War and had to cope with a sometimes ineffective Congress and an undisciplined army. As president, he had to deal with disagreements between the Federalists and the Democratic-Republicans. He also had to watch as issues he defended or favored—for example, the Jay Treaty, a national university, the proclamation of neutrality—were ridiculed, attacked, or dismissed by his enemies. He was even accused of acting like a king. During his final retirement at Mount Vernon,

Washington felt somewhat defensive. He was no longer certain about the state of the country and his place in history. When he was commissioned to serve his country as commander in chief in 1798, Washington signed on out of loyalty to his country and perhaps because he liked feeling needed. When it was suggested that he run for a third presidential term, Washington declined. He knew times had changed, and he might not win. To the end, Washington considered reputation and honor first.

But Washington never felt defeated. He was a self-made man and was constantly motivated by new ideas. He read about politics, literature, law, geography, travel, and most importantly, agriculture. He wrote often to others to exchange ideas and to learn from them. He promoted and helped finance a solid education for his stepchildren, grandchildren, nieces and nephews, and the children of friends. He attended the theater regularly. He struggled to start a national university and a military academy. He supported two schools. In his will, he insisted that his younger slaves be taught to read and write. At the time of his death, Washington's library was filled with nine hundred volumes, many on practical subjects.

As an older man, Washington was in tune with what was going on in the country and was constantly improving things at Mount Vernon. His house was almost always filled with people and lively conversation. Active throughout his life, he made daily rounds of his farms up to the day before he died. And even on that day he went outside to check on some trees.

Washington was a man who became a hero early in life and remained one for the rest of his life. Washington is still a hero, a man—not a superhuman one—who was passionately dedicated to the character and condition of his country.

I hope you enjoy getting to know George Washington.

CHAPTER ONE

THE YOUNG OFFICER

Washington's interest in maps and geography stemmed from his early career as a surveyor.

SURVEYING TRIP, 1748

In 1748, JUST AFTER HE HAD TURNED SIXTEEN, Washington, along with his friend George William Fairfax and surveyor James Genn, traveled to the Shenandoah Valley and the South Branch of the Potomac River on Virginia's frontier to survey land for Lord Fairfax, George Fairfax's relative. Lord Fairfax owned more than five million acres of land in northern Virginia—known as the Northern Neck. This was Washington's first trip to the wilderness. It prepared him well for future trips to the untamed Ohio Valley as a messenger for Lieutenant Governor Dinwiddie, as an officer in the Virginia regiment, and as a volunteer aide in the Braddock campaign. Washington also relied on his knowledge of the wilderness—how to survive and fight there—as commander in chief of the Continental army.

Before 1748, Washington was already surveying land, using his father's instruments. A year after his trip for Lord Fairfax, Washington was made the official surveyor of Culpeper County. He could now earn good money and buy land. In a few years Washington owned more than one thousand acres in the Shenandoah Valley. At his death, he owned about eighty thousand acres of land and titles to lots in a few Virginia cities and in Washington, D.C.

TUESDAY, MARCH 15

We set out early with Intent to Run round the sd. Land but being taken in a Rain & it Increasing very fast obliged us to return. It clearing about one oClock & our time being too Precious to Loose we a second time ventured out & Worked hard till Night & then returned to Penningtons we got our Suppers & was Lighted in to a Room & I not being so good a Woodsman as the rest of my Company striped my self very orderly & went in to the Bed as they call'd it when to my Surprize I found it to be nothing but a Little Straw—Matted together without Sheets or any thing else but only one Thread Bear blanket with double its Weight of Vermin such as Lice Fleas &c. I was glad to get up (as soon as the Light was carried from us) & put on my Cloths & Lay as my Companions. Had we not have been very tired, I am sure we should not have slep'd much that night. I made a Promise not to Sleep so from that time forward chusing rather to sleep in the open Air before a fire as will Appear hereafter.

MEMORANDUM, 1749–1750

As a young man, Washington spent much time with his half brother Lawrence at Mount Vernon in Virginia, where he adopted the aristocratic lifestyle of a country gentleman. Life at Ferry Farm, where he lived with his mother, sister, and brothers, was far from elegant. Life with Lawrence and at Colonel William Fairfax's* nearby estate, Belvoir, however, was filled with formal balls, fancy dinners, public gatherings, hunting parties, and lively

---

*George William's father and cousin to Lord Fairfax

debates. An excellent horseman and dancer, Washington was right at home.

Washington was preoccupied with "civilized" behavior, copying more than a hundred rules on the subject into his school notebook. Throughout his lifetime, he recognized the value of a solid reputation, good manners, education, and proper attire. Washington was just as meticulous about his army uniforms, even designing some, and the velvet suits he wore later in life as he was about the coat he ordered in his late teens.

> Memorandom to have my Coat made by the following Directions to be made a Frock with a Lapel Breast the Lapel to Contain on each side six Button Holes and to be about 5 or 6 Inches wide all the way equal and to turn as the Breast on the Coat does to have it made very Long Waisted and in Length to come down to or below the Bent of the knee the Waist from the armpit to the Fold to be exactly as long or Longer than from thence to the Bottom not to have more than one fold in the Skirt and the top to be made just to turn in and three Button Holes the Lapel at the top to turn as the Cape of the Coat and Bottom to Come Parrallel with the Button Holes the Last Button hole in the Breast to be right opposite to the Button on the Hip.

JOURNAL ENTRY, DECEMBER 1753 (EXCERPT)

Washington made plans not only to better his social and political skills but also to become a great soldier. He was inspired by Lawrence's role as a captain during the Cartagena campaign in the War of Jenkins' Ear between England and Spain.* After Lawrence's death in 1752, Washington was appointed adjutant in one of Virginia's four military districts.

Fiercely ambitious, Washington saw his chance to make his military mark in 1753. At this time, the British were worried about the French, who had set up forts near Lake Erie in the Ohio Valley, land claimed by England. The British also were worried that the French would travel farther south into the valley, take possession of the Ohio River, and establish more forts. Washington volunteered to travel through the wilderness to deliver Britain's message to get out. Guide Christopher Gist, interpreter Jacob Van

---

The war broke out in 1739 and continued into 1740, gradually dissolving into the War of the Austrian Succession.

Braam, four men who took care of the horses and supplies, and Indians who considered the French the enemy accompanied him. Washington was successful—he delivered the message—but the French had no intention of leaving. Washington needed to get back to Williamsburg, Virginia, fast to tell Governor Robert Dinwiddie the bad news. Unfortunately, the trip was long, dangerous, and filled with many hardships.

The Day following, just after we had pass'd a Place call'd the Murdering Town where we intended to quit the Path & steer across the Country for Shanapins Town, we fell in with a Party of French Indians, which had laid in wait for us, one of them fired at Mr. Gist or me, not 15 Steps, but fortunately missed. We took this Fellow into Custody, & kept him 'till about 9 o'Clock at Night, & then let him go, & then walked all the remaining Part of the Night without making any Stop; that we might get the start, so far as to be out of the reach of their Pursuit next Day, as were well assur'd they wou'd follow upon our Tract as soon as it was Light: The next Day we continued traveling 'till it was quite Dark, & got to the River about two Miles above Shanapins; we expected to have found the River Froze, but it was not, only about 50 Yards from each Shoar; the Ice I suppose had broke up above, for it was driving in vast Quantities.

There was no way for us to get over but upon a Raft, which we set about with but one poor Hatchet, & got finish'd just after Sunsetting, after a whole days Work: We got it launch'd, & on board of it, & sett off; but before we got half over, we were jamed in the Ice in such a Manner, that we expected every Moment our Raft wou'd sink, & we Perish; I put out my seting Pole, to try to stop the Raft, that the Ice might pass by, when the Rapidity of the Stream through it with so much Violence against the Pole, that it Jirk'd me into 10 Feet Water, but I fortunately saved my Self by catching hold of one of the Raft Logs. Notwithstanding all our Efforts we cou'd not get the Raft to either Shoar, but were oblig'd, as we were pretty near an Island, to quit our Raft & wade to it. The Cold was so extream severe, that Mr. Gist got all his Fingers, & some of his Toes Froze, & the Water was shut up so hard, that We found no Difficulty in getting off the Island on the Ice in the Morning, & went to Mr. Frazers.

After the rafting experience on the Allegheny River (left), Washington traveled to the mouth of the Youghiogheny River to visit Queen Aliquippa, a Seneca leader of an Indian community and friend to the English. Washington presented her with a match coat (an outer garment) and a bottle of rum (below). These illustrations are from books published more than one hundred years ago.

To John Augustine Washington, *May 31, 1754*
From Camp in the Great Meadows, Pennsylvania

When Washington returned from his trip to the Ohio frontier, his journal was published. It was also printed in many colonial newspapers and in London, making people aware not only of the intentions of the French but also of George Washington.

Governor Dinwiddie soon sent Washington back to the Ohio Valley to stop the French invasion. On May 28, Lieutenant Colonel Washington and a small troop of soldiers were involved in a minor skirmish with the French that ignited the French and Indian War. Although the following letter to his younger brother "Jack" suggests that Washington enjoyed combat, he most likely enjoyed being a soldier "serving his country." Washington continued to serve his country throughout his lifetime.

After the skirmish, Washington and his troops built Fort Necessity at Great Meadows. Unfortunately, when the French and their Indian allies counterattacked in early July, the fort provided little or no protection. Surrounded and outnumbered, Washington was forced to surrender. Because of problems in understanding French, Washington and James Mackay, an officer in charge of an independent company of British regulars, signed a document that stated that the French commander, Jumonville, had been assassinated during the May skirmish. The French claimed that Jumonville and his men had been on a diplomatic mission to warn the British to leave the valley, and they were forced to avenge his "murder."

> Dr John
>
> Since my last we have arrived at this place, where 3 days agoe we had an engagemt wth the French that is, between a party of theirs & Ours; Most of our men were out upon other detachments, so that I had scarcely 40 men under my Command, and about 10, or a doz. Indians, nevertheless we obtained a most signal Victory. The Battle lasted abt 10, or 15 minutes, sharp firing on both sides, when the French gave ground & run, but to no great purpose; there were 12 killed, among which was Monsr De Jumonville the Commandr, & taken 21 prisoners with whom are Monsieurs La Force, Druillong, together with 2 Cadets. I have sent them to his Honr the Governor at Winchester conducted by Lieut. West & a guard of 20 men. We

had but one man killed, 2 or 3 wounded and a great many more within an Inch of being shott; among the wounded on our side was Lieut. Waggoner, but no danger will ensue.

We expect every Hour to be attacked by a superior Force, but shall if they stay one day longer be prepared for them; We have already got Intrenchments & are about a Pallisado'd Fort, which will I hope be finished today. The Mingo's* have struck the French & I hope will give a good blow before they have done, I expect 40 odd of them here to night, wch with our Fort and some reinforcements from Colo. Fry,** will enable us to exert our Noble Courage with Spirit. I am Yr Affe Bror

Geo. Washington

I fortunately escaped without a wound, tho' the right Wing where I stood was exposed to & received all the Enemy's fire and was the part where the man was killed & the rest wounded. I can with truth assure you, I heard Bulletts whistle and believe me there was something charming in the sound.

To Colonel William Fitzhugh, November 15, 1754 (EXCERPT) From Belvoir

Colonel Washington returned from Fort Necessity to learn not only that the Virginia regiment had been reorganized into independent companies but also that he had been demoted to captain. A proud Washington obeyed "the call of Honour, and the advice of my Friends" and resigned from the military in October 1754. He would not be humiliated.

Even when it was offered that he could retain his commission as colonel, but with the rank and pay of a provincial captain, he was not persuaded to change his mind. Washington wrote often about the unfair status of provincial officers compared with those who had royal commissions and were part of the British regular army.

But even though he resigned and considered military life unhealthy and dangerous, Washington was now a confirmed soldier. At the end of the letter he admits, "my inclinations are strongly bent to arms." Throughout his life-

---

*Indians

**Colonel Fry led this campaign, with Washington second in command. Although Fry had died on May 31, 1754, Washington did not learn that until early June. He then succeeded Fry as commander with the rank of colonel.

time, Washington stressed, sometimes to the point of complaining, that officers and soldiers were not appreciated. Notice at the end of the following excerpt that he points out the sacrifices he endured while fighting the French at Fort Necessity.

> You make mention in your letter of my continuing in the Service, and retaining my Colo.'s Commission. This idea has filled me with surprise: for if you think me capable of holding a Commission that has neither rank or emolument [compensation] annexed to it; you must entertain a very contemptible opinion of my weakness, and believe me to be more empty than the Commission itself.
>
> Besides, Sir, if I had time, I could enumerate many good reasons, that forbid all thoughts of my Returning; and which, to you, or any other, would, upon the strictest scrutiny, appear to be well-founded. I must be reduced to a very low Command, and subjected to that of many who have acted as my inferior Officers. In short, every Captain, bearing the King's Commission; every half-pay Officer, or other, appearing with such commission, would rank before me; for these reasons, I choose to submit to the loss of Health, which I have, however, already sustained (not to mention that of Effects) and the fatigue I have undergone in our first Efforts; than subject myself to the same inconveniences, and run the risque of a second disappointment. I shall have the consolation itself, of knowing, that I have opened the way when the smallness of our numbers exposed us to the attacks of a Superior Enemy; That I have hitherto stood the heat and brunt of the Day, and escaped untouched, in time of extreme danger; and that I have the Thanks of my Country, for the Services I have rendered it.

TO SARAH CARY FAIRFAX, APRIL 30, 1755 (EXCERPT)
From Bullskin Plantation*

Much has been written about Washington's relationship with his best friend's wife. Perhaps because he was so ambitious, Washington did not have time to form many lasting friendships. He kept a distance from people, even from those who served under him or worked for him. He did this

---

*Washington owned Bullskin Plantation, a tobacco plantation in Frederick County.

intentionally in order to have control over them.

"Sally" and her husband, George William Fairfax, were among Washington's closest friends. More than forty years later, Washington would reflect on his friendship with Sally as "the happiest in my life."

> In order to engage your corrispondance, I think it is incumbent on me to deserve it; which I shall endeavour to do, by embracing the earliest, and every oppertunity, of writing to you.
>
> It will be needless to dwell on the pleasures that a corrispondence of this kind would afford me, let it suffice to say—a corrispondance with my Friends is the greatest satisfaction I expect to enjoy, in the course of the Campaigne,* and that from none shall I derive such satisfaction as from yours— for to you I stand indebted for many Obligations.

TO MARY BALL WASHINGTON, JUNE 7, 1755 (EXCERPT)
From Fort Cumberland, Maryland

Washington and his mother were not close. She complained that he left her often and was not overly concerned with her emotional and financial well-being. He felt that her wants were unrealistic (such as her need for butter and a servant) or unnecessary (such as her constant need for money, which Washington often lent to her). More importantly, she failed to appreciate his goals or recognize his accomplishments.

Mary Ball Washington lived at Ferry Farm and then in a small home in Fredericksburg, Virginia.

> I was favour'd with your Letter by Mr Dick,** and am sorry it is not in my power to provide you with a Dutch Servant, or the Butter agreeably to you[r] desire, We are quite out of that part of the Country where either are to be had, there being few or no Inhabitants where we now lie Encampd, & butter cannot be had here to supply the wants of the army.
>
> I am sorry it was not in my power to call upon you as I went to, or returned from Williamsburg The business I went upon, (viz: money for the army), woud not suffer an hour's delay.

---

*Washington was involved in the Braddock campaign from March–July 1755 (see pages 22–24).
**a merchant

Mary Ball grew up in Virginia and lost both of her parents at an early age. On March 6, 1731, at the age of twenty-three, Mary Ball married Augustine Washington. He died in 1743, and Mary never married again.

TO MARY BALL WASHINGTON, JULY 18, 1755
From Fort Cumberland, Maryland

Washington returned to military life in 1755 as a volunteer aide to British Major General Edward Braddock. Braddock was brought to America to lead regular and provincial troops against the French. His mission was to attack Fort Duquesne, the French fort in the Ohio Valley, and force the French from the area. Unfortunately, the campaign failed. Braddock was ambushed, his column routed, and he was killed. In this letter to his mother, Washington blames the British regulars as cowards and points to the bravery of the provincials, particularly his fellow Virginians.

Washington was applauded in both America and England for his courage during the Braddock campaign. The fact that he survived was considered a miracle. Although the public knew Washington after his first wilderness journeys in 1753 and 1754, he now returned a hero. Almost immediately Washington became commander of all Virginia's military forces.

To Mrs Washington

Honour'd Madm

As I doubt not but you have heard of our defeat, and perhaps have had it represented in a worse light (if possible) than it deserves; I have taken this earliest oppertunity to give you some acct of the Engagement, as it happen'd within 7 miles of the French Fort on Wednesday the 9th Inst.

We Marchd onto that place witht any considerable loss, havg only now and then a stragler pickd up by the French Scoutg Indns. When we came there, we were attackd by a body of French and Indns whose number (I am persuaded) did not exceed 300 Men; our's consisted of abt 1,300 well armd Troops; *chiefly* Regular Soldiers, who were struck with such a panick, that they behavd with more cowardice than it is possible to conceive; The Officers behav'd Gallantly in order to encourage their Men, for which they sufferd greatly; there being near 60 killd and wounded; a large proportion out of the number we had! The Virginia Troops shewd a good deal of Bravery, & were near all killd; for I believe out of 3 Companys that were there, their is scarce 30 Men left alive; Capt. Peyrouny & all his Officer's down to a Corporal was killd; Capt. Polson shard near as hard a Fate, for only one of his was left: In short the dastardly behaviour of thos<e> they call regular's, exposd all other's that were inclind to do their duty to almost certain death; and at last, in dispight of all the efforts of the Officer's to the Contrary, they broke, and run as Sheep pursued by dogs; and it was impossible to rally them. The Genl was wounded; of wch he died 3 Days after; Sir Peter Halket was killd in the Field: where died many other brave Officer's; I luckily escapd witht a wound, tho' I had four Bullets through my Coat, and two Horses shot under me; Captns Orme & Morris two of the Aids de Camps, were wounded early in the Engagemt which renderd the duty harder upon me, as I was the only person then left to distribute the Genls Orders, which I was scarcely able to do, as I was not half recoverd from a violent illness that had confin'd me to my Bed, and a Waggon, for above 10 days; I am still in a weak

---

Angled brackets are used to indicate mutilated or illegible letters or words in the original document.

and Feeble condn which induces me to halt here 2 or 3 Days in hopes of recovg a little Strength, to enable me to proceed homewards; from whence, I fear I shall not be able to stir till towards Sepr, so that I shall not have the pleasure of seeing you till then, unless it be in Fairfax; please to give my love [to] Mr Lewis and my Sister, & Compts to Mr Jackson and all other Fds that enquire after me. I am Hond Madm Yr most Dutiful Son

G.W——n

P.S. You may acqt Priscilla Mullican that her Son Charles is very well, havg only recd a slight wd in his Foot wch will be curd witht detrimt to him in a very small time. We had abt 300 Men killd and as many, <o>r more, wounded: and this chiefly done by our own Men.

CHAPTER TWO

VIRGINIA'S COMMANDER

Colonel Washington at the age of 25

TO MARY BALL WASHINGTON, AUGUST 14, 1755

From Mount Vernon

BOUND BY DUTY AND HONOR, Washington accepted the command of the Virginia forces, despite his mother's wishes, two weeks after writing this letter.

> To Mrs Washington
> Honourd Madam
>   If it is in my power to avoid going to the Ohio again, I shall, but if the Command is press'd upon me by the genl voice of the Country, and offerd upon such terms as can't be objected

against, it woud reflect dishonour upon me to refuse it; and that I am sure must, or ought, to give you greater cause of uneasiness than my going in an honourable Comd; for upon no other terms I will accept of it, at present I have no proposals, made to me nor have any advice of such an intention except from private hands. I am Dr Mm &c.

TO JOHN CAMPBELL, EARL OF LOUDOUN, JANUARY 10, 1757 (EXCERPTS)
From Fort Cumberland, Maryland

As commander of the Virginia Regiment, Washington often complained to authorities that his troops were undisciplined, discontented, lacking in strength and number, underpaid, and most importantly, ill equipped. Washington would repeat these same complaints when he took over the Continental Army. He often wrote Congress about the value of the army, demanding that officers and soldiers receive fair pay, good training, and adequate equipment and supplies.

In his letter to his commander, the Earl of Loudoun, Washington provides a history of the "unhappy Situation" of his troops. He insists that strict rules need to be put into effect in order to regulate the troops and protect and defend the "extensive" frontier.

Washington also points out that it was expected that the regiment would be incorporated into the regular British army and that he was promised a royal commission by Braddock. Washington also believed that William Shirley, the commander in charge after Braddock, supported regular commissions for provincial officers.

Loudoun did not incorporate the regiment into the regular army or grant Washington a royal commission. As a result, Washington's anti-British feelings began to take root.

To the Right Honourable The Earl of Loudoun, General, and Commander in Chief of all His Majesty's Forces in North America. and Governor, and Commander in Chief of His Majesty's most Ancient Colony and Dominion of Virginia.

In regard to myself, I must beg leave to say, Had His

Excellency General Braddock survived his unfortunate Defeat, I should have met with preferment equal to my Wishes: I had His Promise to that purpose, and I believe that Gentleman was too sincere and generous to make unmeaning offers, where none were ask'd. General Shirley was not unkind in His Promises—but—He is gone to England.

I don't know My Lord, in what light this plain and disinterested relation of our Circumstances may be received by Your Lordship, but with the utmost candour and Submission it is offer'd. It contains no aggravated Circumstances, nor unjust Reflections.

Virginia is a Country young in War. Untill the breaking out of these Disturbances has Lived in the most profound, and Tranquil Peace; never studying War or Warfare. It is not therefore to be imagined She can fall into proper Measures at once. All that can be expected at Her Hands She chearfully gives. The Sinews of War. And we only want a Person of your Lordship's Ability and Experience to direct the Application. It is for this Reason, I have presumed to hint these Grievances: That if any thing in them appear worthy of Redress, & Your Lordship will condescend to point out the way; it may be Obtained.

When I look over the Preceeding Pages and find, how far I have exceeded my first Intention, I blush with shame to think of my Freedom. Nothing My Lord, but an Affectionate Zeal to Serve my Country, Steady Attachment to Her Interest, The Honour of Her Arms, and crying Grievances which She is labourg under can plead an Excuse, Untill I am happy enough to have an opportunity of Testifying, with what Profound Respect I have the Honour to be, My Lord, Your Lordship's Most Obedient, and Most Humble Servant,

Go: Washington

To Sarah Cary Fairfax, September 12, 1758 (Excerpt)
From Camp at Fort Cumberland

It is not known if Washington and Martha Custis were engaged by September 1758. Many historians feel that Washington is not revealing his feelings about his future wife in this letter but secretly admitting his love for Sally Fairfax. Washington and Martha married four months later, and Martha soon became close friends of Sally and her husband.

Tis true, I profess myself a Votary to Love—I acknowledge that a Lady is in the Case—and further I confess, that this Lady is known to you.—Yes Madam, as well as she is to one, who is too sensible of her Charms to deny the Power, whose Influence he feels and must ever Submit to. I feel the force of her amiable beauties in the recollection of a thousand tender passages that I coud wish to obliterate, till I am bid to revive them.—but experience alas! sadly reminds me how Impossible this is.—and evinces an Opinion which I have long entertaind, that there is a Destiny, which has the Sovereign controul of our Actions—not to be resisted by the strongest efforts of Human Nature.

You have drawn me my dear Madam, or rather have I drawn myself, into an honest confession of a Simple Fact—misconstrue not my meaning—'tis obvious—doubt it not, nor expose it,—the World has no business to know the object of my Love, declard in this manner to—you when I want to conceal it—One thing, above all things in this World I wish to know, and only one person of your Acquaintance can solve me that, or guess my meaning.—but adieu to this, till happier times, if I ever shall see them.—the hours at present are melancholy dull.—neither the rugged Toils of War, nor the gentler conflict of A——B—s [Assembly Balls] is in my choice.—I dare believe you are as happy as you say—I wish I was happy also—Mirth, good Humour, ease of Mind and.—what else? cannot fail to render you so; and consummate your Wishes.

TO THE OFFICERS OF THE VIRGINIA REGIMENT, JANUARY 10, 1759
From New Kent County

Washington resigned his command in December 1758. Shortly afterwards, his officers prepared an address to him. Throughout his military career, Washington was known for the respect he earned from those who served under him. The officers refer to Washington as an "excellent Commander," a "sincere Friend," an "affable" "Companion," the "Soul of the whole Corps" and a man "renown'd for Patriotism, Courage and Conduct." They did not want Washington to resign.

Although Washington's years as Virginia's commander did not bring him as much glory as he had hoped, he left the regiment with his honor and reputation firmly intact. This is evident in his response to the officers of the Virginia Regiment. Throughout the country, Washington remained the brave young officer from Virginia.

To Captain Robert Steward and Gentlemen Officers of the Virginia Regiment.

My dear Gentlemen.

If I had words that could express the deep sense I entertain of your most obliging & affectionate address to me, I should endeavour to shew you that *gratitude* is not the smallest engredient of a character you have been pleased to celebrate; rather, give me leave to add, as the effect of your partiality & politeness, than of my deserving.

That I have for some years (under uncommon difficulties, which few were thoroughly acquainted with) been able to conduct myself so much to your satisfaction, affords <me> the greatest pleasure I am capable of feeling; as I almost despared of attaining that end—so hard a matter is it to please, when one is acting under disagreeable restraints! But your having, nevertheless, so fully, so affectionately & so publicly declared your approbation of my conduct, during my command of the Virginia Troops, I must esteem an honor that will constitute the greatest happiness of my life, and afford in my latest hours the most pleasing reflections. I had nothing to boast, but a steady honesty—this I made the invariable rule of my actions; and I find my reward in it.

I am bound, Gentlemen, in honor, by inclination & by every affectionate tye, to promote the reputation & interest of a Corps I was once a member of; though the Fates have disjoined me from it now, I beseech you to command, with equal confidence & a greater degree of freedom than ever, my best services. Your Address is in the hands of the Governor, and will be presented by him to the Council. I hope (but cannot ascertain it) that matters may be settled agreeable to your wishes. On me, depend for my best endeavours to accomplish this end.

I should dwell longer on this subject, and be more particular in my answer, did your address lye before me. Permit me then to conclude with the following acknowledgments: first, that I always thought it, as it really was, the greatest honor of my life to command Gentlemen, who made me happy in their company & easy by their conduct: secondly, that had every thing contributed as fully as your obliging endeavours did to render me satisfied, I never should have been otherwise, or have had cause to know the pangs I have felt at parting with a Regiment, that has shared my toils, and experienced every hardship & danger, which I have encountered. But this brings on *reflections* that fill me with grief & I must strive to forget them; in thanking you, Gentlemen, with uncommon sincerity & true affection for the honor you have done me—for if I have acquired any reputation, it is from you I derive it. I thank you also for the love & regard you have all along shewn me. It is in this, I am rewarded. It is herein I glory. And lastly I must thank you for your kind wishes. To assure you, that I feel every generous return of mutual regard—that I wish you every honor as a collective Body & every felicity in your private Characters, is, Gentlemen, I hope unnecessary—Shew me how I can demonstrate it, and you never shall find me otherwise than your Most obedient, most obliged and most affectionate

Go. Washington.

CHAPTER THREE

FARMER, FAMILY MAN, BUSINESSMAN, AND STATESMAN

In the late 1750s, Washington courted Martha Dandridge Custis, a widow with two small children, Jacky and Patsy. When they married on January 6, 1759, Martha was twenty-seven and Washington twenty-six.

TO RICHARD WASHINGTON, SEPTEMBER 20, 1759 (EXCERPT)

From Mount Vernon

HISTORIANS HAVE QUESTIONED whether Washington married Martha Custis for love or because she had money, property, and land. The following letter to a merchant and perhaps a relative, which Washington wrote about nine months after his marriage, does not offer any clues. But Washington and Martha were devoted partners, married for more than forty years.

Washington dances the minuet with his close friend Sally Fairfax.

One letter from Martha to Washington and two letters from Washington to his wife survive (see pages 39–41). Martha destroyed almost all of their correspondence, keeping the true nature of their relationship private.

> I am now I beleive fixd at this Seat with an agreable Consort for Life and hope to find more happiness in retirement than I ever experiencd amidst a wide and bustling World . . .

DIARY ENTRY, FEBRUARY 15, 1760 (EXCERPT)

From Mount Vernon, Washington often traveled to nearby Alexandria, Virginia, for business and pleasure. He also traveled to Virginia's capital, Williamsburg, to attend meetings of the House of Burgesses and to take in card games, dances, teas, and theater.

Washington greatly enjoyed dancing. On one occasion during the Revolutionary War, he danced for more than three hours with Catharine "Kitty" Greene, the wife of one of his officers.

As with almost everything else, Washington had high standards for formal balls and dinners. This one obviously did not meet his approval.

The First Gentleman of Virginia by John Ward Dunsmore (1856–1945), oil on canvas, 1909. Washington was strong, athletic, and fond of exercise. He especially loved fox hunting.

Went to a Ball at Alexandria—where Musick and Dancing was the chief Entertainment. However in a convenient Room detachd for the purpose abounded great plenty of Bread and Butter, some Biscuets with Tea, & Coffee which the Drinkers of coud not Distinguish from Hot water sweetned. Be it remembered that pocket handkerchiefs servd the purposes of Table Cloths & Napkins and that no Apologies were made for either. I shall therefore distinguish this Ball by the Stile & title of the Bread & Butter Ball.

TO GEORGE MASON, APRIL 5, 1769 (EXCERPT)
From Mount Vernon

Washington and George Mason were members of the House of Burgesses, neighbors, fellow fox hunters, farmers, and good friends. They also saw eye to eye on the high taxes imposed by the British. Later, tensions erupted between the two men during the writing and ratification of the Constitution. Mason supported a bill of rights, which did not at first accompany the Constitution, and refused to sign and support it. Washington, on the other hand, promoted the Constitution and quietly campaigned to have it ratified. The two men were not close after the late 1780s.

Here Washington discusses implementing an effective plan to convince England of America's right to certain liberties. He admits that addresses and protests have not worked and recommends forming a nonimportation association in Virginia. He even promotes using force if all else fails, a revolutionary thought at the time.

Mason lent his support and drafted a plan for a Virginia nonimportation association,* which Washington brought up at the meeting of the Assembly in May. The association was formed but was dissolved two years later, after England had repealed the Townshend Acts.

> At a time when our lordly Masters in Great Britain will be satisfied with nothing less than the deprivation of American freedom, it seems highly necessary that something shou'd be done to avert the stroke and maintain the liberty which we have derived from our Ancestors; but the manner of doing it to answer the purpose effectually is the point in question.
>
> That no man shou'd scruple, or hesitate a moment to use a—ms in defence of so valuable a blessing, on which all the good and evil of life depends; is clearly my opinion; Yet A—ms I wou'd beg leave to add, should be the last resource; the de[r]nier resort. Addresses to the Throne, and remonstrances to parliament, we have already, it is said, proved the inefficacy of; how far then their attention to our rights & priviledges is to be awakened or alarmed by starving their Trade & manufactures, remains to be tryed.

TO JONATHAN BOUCHER, DECEMBER 16, 1770
From Mount Vernon

Washington and Martha never had children, but Washington was stepfather to Martha "Patsy" Parke Custis and John "Jacky" Parke Custis, Martha's children from her first marriage. Patsy and Jacky were very young when Washington and Martha married. Washington helped raise them

---

The colony would not import or purchase taxed goods and other products from Great Britain until the Townshend Acts, which placed duties on certain goods, were repealed.

and made sure they received a good education. He also ordered toys, clothes, books, and musical instruments for them from England.

Washington was closer to Patsy than to Jacky, who he felt was undisciplined. Washington wrote often to Jonathan Boucher, who ran a school in Annapolis, Maryland, that Jacky attended, about the young man's need for good manners, reputation, and education. He also worried that Jacky would be corrupted by life in the "big city" of Annapolis.

Revd Sir,

According to appointment Jacky Custis now returns to Annapolis—His Mind a good deal relaxed from Study, & more than ever turnd to Dogs Horses & Guns; indeed upon Dress & equipage, which till of late, he has discoverd little Inclination of giving into. I must beg the favour of you therefore to keep him close to those useful branches of Learning which he ought now to be acquainted with, & as much as possible, under your own Eye. without these, I fear he will too soon think himself above controul, & be not much the better for the extraordinary expence attending his Living in Annapolis, which I shoud be exceeding sorry for, as nothing but a hasty progress towards the completion of his Education, can justifie my keeping him there at such an expence as his Estate will now become chargeable with.

The time of Life he is now advancing into requires the most friendly aid and Council (especially in such a place as Annapolis); otherwise, the warmth of his own Passions, assisted by the bad example of other Youth, may prompt him to Actions derogatory of Virtue, & that Innocence of Manners which one coud wish to preserve him in: For wch reason I woud beg leave to request, that, he may not be suffered to Sleep from under your own Roof, unless it be at such places as you are sure he can have no bad examples set him; nor allow him to be rambling about at Nights in Company with those, who do not care how debauchd and vicious his Conduct may be.

You will be so good I hope, as to excuse the liberty I have taken in offering my Sentiments thus freely—I have his welbeing much at Heart, & shoud be sorry to see him fall into any vice, or evil course, which there is a possibility of restraining him from. With very great esteem I remain Revd Sir Yr Most Hble Servt

Go: Washington

TO BURWELL BASSETT*
JUNE 20, 1773 (EXCERPT)
From Mount Vernon

Washington had hoped that Patsy would become a planter's wife, but she suffered from epilepsy and died suddenly at the age of seventeen.

Dear Sir

It is an easier matter to conceive, than to describe, the distress of this Family; especially that of the unhappy Parent of our Dear Patcy Custis, when I inform you that yesterday removd the Sweet Innocent Girl into a more happy, & peaceful abode than any she has met with, in the afflicted Path she hitherto has trod.

She rose from Dinner about four Oclock, in better health and spirits than she appeard to have been in for some time; soon after which she was siezd with one of her usual Fits, & expird in it, in less than two Minutes without uttering a Word, a groan, or scarce a Sigh.—this Sudden, and unexpected blow, I scarce need add has almost reduced my poor Wife to the lowest ebb of Misery; which is encreas'd by the absence of her Son . . . and want of the balmy Consolation of her Relations . . .

Washington's brother–in–law

CHAPTER FOUR

COMMANDER IN CHIEF OF THE AMERICAN FORCES

ADDRESS TO THE CONTINENTAL CONGRESS, PHILADELPHIA, JUNE 16, 1775

WASHINGTON'S EXPERIENCE HAD NOT EXACTLY qualified him to command the American forces. He had led only small units in wilderness campaigns, was not a trained officer, and did not have a firm grasp of military tactics and strategies. Despite these weaknesses, Washington knew how to deal with others. Throughout his early military career, he had petitioned and negotiated with royal officials and officers. His experience with the House of Burgesses and the Continental Congresses furthered his negotiating skills. These skills would prove invaluable during the Revolutionary War.

Washington also was from Virginia, which helped. The appointment of a Virginian would draw that colony—and other southern colonies—closer to the cause.

Despite his hesitations, Washington wanted the command. He often showed up at the meetings of the Second Continental Congress in a military uniform he had designed himself. But Washington worried about failing. After he was given the appointment, he told Patrick Henry that it would "'date my fall, and the ruin of my reputation.'"

Washington was not the only person considered for the post of commander in chief. Some delegates felt that the position should go to Artemas Ward, a New Englander who was in charge of troops in Massachusetts, while others favored Charles Lee, a retired British officer who now lived in America. But when it came time to elect a commander, Washington was the unanimous choice.

When Washington refused a salary and requested that only his expenses be paid, the delegates were pleased with their decision. His reputation as a man of noble character was firmly in place.

Mr President, Tho' I am truly sensible of the high Honour done me in this Appointment, yet I feel great distress, from a consciousness that my abilities & Military experience may not be equal to the extensive & important Trust: However, as the Congress desire i<t> I will enter upon the momentous duty, & exert every power I Possess In their service & for the Support of the glorious Cause: I beg they will accept my most cordial thanks for this distinguished testimony of their Approbation.

But lest some unlucky event should happen unfavourable to my reputation, I beg it may be rememberd by every Gentn in the room, that I this day declare with the utmost sincerity, I do not think my self equal to the Command I <am> honoured with.

As to pay, Sir, I beg leave to Assure the Congress that as no pecuniary consideration could have tempted me to have accepted this Arduous emploiment at the expence of my domestk ease & happi<ness> I do not wish to make any proffit from it: I will keep an exact Account of my expences; those I doubt not they will discharge & that is all I desire.

Dark-haired and only five feet tall, Martha Dandridge was born in
1731 and grew up in Virginia. At eighteen, she married Daniel
Parke Custis, a planter, and had four children. Two died as infants.

Two Letters to Martha

June 18, 1775 (Excerpt)
From Philadelphia

In this letter, Washington is not completely candid, telling Martha that
he used "every endeavour in my power to avoid" the commission.

Character, honor, and reputation were often the reasons Washington
gave when making important decisions. Here he also refers to
"Providence," which protected him in past battles and makes him confident
that the war will be short. Unfortunately, the war lasted eight years.
Washington returned to Mount Vernon for only two short visits during the
war, but he and Martha were often together. She joined him in Cambridge,

Massachusetts, in December 1775 and visited him at winter encampments throughout the war.

This letter is often compared to Washington's letter of August 14, 1755, to his mother (see pages 25–26). Washington's ambition to serve his country and make a name for himself was perhaps more important than anything else—including family.

My Dearest,

I am now set down to write to you on a subject which fills me with inexpressable concern—and this concern is greatly aggravated and Increased when I reflect on the uneasiness I know it will give you—It has been determined in Congress, that the whole Army raised for the defence of the American Cause shall be put under my care, and that it is necessary for me to proceed immediately to Boston to take upon me the Command of it. You may beleive me my dear Patcy, when I assure you, in the most solemn manner, that, so far from seeking this appointment I have used every endeavour in my power to avoid it, not only from my unwillingness to part with you and the Family, but from a consciousness of its being a trust too great for my Capacity and that I should enjoy more real happiness and felicity in one month with you, at home, than I have the most distant prospect of reaping abroad, if my stay was to be Seven times Seven years. But, as it has been a kind of destiny that has thrown me upon this Service, I shall hope that my undertaking of it, is designd to answer some good purpose—You might, and I suppose did perceive, from the Tenor of my letters, that I was apprehensive I could not avoid this appointment, as I did not even pretend <t>o intimate when I should return—that was the case—it was utterly out of my power to refuse this appointment without exposing my Character to such censures as would have reflected dishonour upon myself, and given pain to my friends—this I am sure could not, and ought not to be pleasing to you, & must have lessend me considerably in my own esteem. I shall rely therefore, confidently, on that Providence which has heretofore preservd, & been bountiful to me, not doubting but that I shall return safe to you in the fall—I shall feel no pain from the Toil, or the danger of the Campaign—My unhappiness will flow, from the uneasiness I know you will feel at being left alone—I therefore beg of you to summon your whole fortitude & Resolution, and pass your time as agreeably as possible—nothing will give me so much sincere satisfaction as to hear this, and to hear it from your own Pen.

JUNE 23, 1775
From Philadelphia

My dearest,

As I am within a few Minutes of leaving this City, I could not think of departing from it without dropping you a line; especially as I do not know whether it may be in my power to write again till I get to the Camp at Boston—I go fully trusting in that Providence, which has been more bountiful to me than I deserve, & in full confidence of a happy meeting with you sometime in the Fall—I have not time to add more, as I am surrounded with Company to take leave of me—I retain an unalterable affection for you, which neither time or distance can change, my best love to Jack & Nelly,* & regard for the rest of the Family concludes me with the utmost truth & sincerety Yr entire

Go: Washington

This map of the "thirteen states of 1776" was printed in a book published in 1905.

---

*Washington's stepson and his wife, Eleanor Calvert Custis

On July 9, 1776, five days after the Declaration of Independence was adopted, George Washington had it read to his troops in New York.

General Orders, Headquarters, New York, August 1, 1776

Five days after the Declaration of Independence was adopted on July 4, 1776, Washington had the document read to his troops in New York. If Washington worried that it would not be well received, he was pleasantly surprised. He wrote to John Hancock, president of the Continental Congress, on July 10, "I caused the Declaration to be proclaimed before all the Army under my Immediate command and have the pleasure to inform them that the measure seemed to have their most hearty assent, The expressions and behavior both of Officers and men testifying their warmest approbation of It."

The Americans were now fighting for independence and not some sort of compromise. The army, which initially had been largely made up of New England forces, was now filled with men of many "Nations, Countries, and Provinces."

It was a hard time for Washington. There was much sickness and unrest among the combined troops, and desertion was high. Many soldiers and officers felt helpless when they saw the huge number of British ships sitting in New York's waters and their military forces on land. Washington promoted unity and harmony in order to build a successful national army.

Parole Paris.   Countersign Reading.

It is with great concern, the General understands, that Jealousies &c: are arisen among the troops from the different Provinces, of reflections frequently thrown out, which can only tend to irritate each other, and injure the noble cause in which we are engaged, and which we ought to support with one hand and one heart. The General most earnestly entreats the officers, and soldiers, to consider the consequences; that they can no way assist our cruel enemies more effectually, than making division among ourselves; That the Honor and Success of the army, and the safety of our bleeding Country, depends upon harmony and good agreement with each other; That the Provinces are all United to oppose the common enemy, and all distinctions sunk in the name of an American; to make this honorable, and preserve the Liberty of our Country, ought to be our only emulation, and he will be the best Soldier, and the best Patriot, who contributes most to this glorious work, whatever his Station, or from whatever part of the Continent, he may come: Let all distinctions of Nations, Countries, and Provinces, therefore be lost in the generous contest, who shall behave with the most Courage against the enemy, and the most kindness and good humour to each other—If there are any officers, or soldiers, so lost to virtue and a love of their Country as to continue in such practices after this order; The General assures them, and is directed by Congress to declare, to the whole Army, that such persons shall be severely punished and dismissed the service with disgrace.

To Lund Washington, September 30, 1776 (excerpt)
From Col. Morris's* on the Heights of Harlem

Washington often confided in his cousin Lund Washington, who was taking care of Mount Vernon during his absence. Although a portion of this letter is devoted to Washington's concerns about Mount Vernon, most of the letter shows how frustrating and humiliating the war could be for him at times.

Washington had just suffered a major defeat at the Battle of Long Island in late August. Three weeks later his troops were forced to flee Kip's Bay and retreat to Harlem Heights in New York.

In Harlem Heights, Washington worried not only about the advancing British army but also about the state of his army, a large part of which was made up of the militia and other short-term units supplied by the states. Washington felt that the militia was undisciplined and indifferent, often packing up and returning home as soon as, if not before, their enlistments were up. Washington desperately wanted to command a large, reliable army of soldiers and officers with longer enlistments. Under these circumstances a "wearied" Washington was in a no-win situation. He could not serve "with reputation"; nor could he resign without causing "inevitable ruin."

In short, such is my situation that if I were to wish the bitterest curse to an enemy on this side of the grave, I should put him in my stead with my feelings; and yet I do not know what plan of conduct to pursue. I see the impossibility of serving with rep-

*Colonel Roger Morris's home was used as headquarters.

44

utation, or doing any essential service to the cause by continuing in command, and yet I am told that if I quit the command inevitable ruin will follow from the distraction that will ensue. In confidence I tell you that I never was in such an unhappy, divided state since I was born. To lose all comfort and happiness on the one hand, whilst I am fully persuaded that under such a system of management as has been adopted, I cannot have the least chance for reputation, nor those allowances made which the nature of the case requires; and to be told, on the other, that if I leave the service all will be lost, is, at the same time that I am bereft of every peaceful moment, distressing to a degree. But I will be done with the subject, with the precaution to you that it is not a fit one to be publicly known or discussed. If I fall, it may not be amiss that these circumstances be known, and declaration made in credit to the justice of my character. And if the men will stand by me (which by the by I despair of), I am resolved not to be forced from this ground while I have life; and a few days will determine the point, if the enemy should not change their plan of operations; for they certainly will not—I am sure they ought not—to waste the season that is now fast advancing, and must be precious to them. I thought to have given you a more explicit account of my situation, expectation, and feelings, but I have not time. I am wearied to death all day with a variety of perplexing circumstances—disturbed at the conduct of the militia, whose behavior and want of discipline has done great injury to the other troops, who never had officers, except in a few instances, worth the bread they eat. My time, in short, is so much engrossed that I have not leisure for corresponding, unless it is on mere matters of public business.

TO SIR WILLIAM HOWE, OCTOBER 6, 1777

Even though he was preoccupied with fighting a war, Washington made sure that General Howe's dog was returned to him. The enemy commander's dog had been picked up between the lines by Continental soldiers. The Revolutionary War has been called the last war between gentlemen, and Washington's gesture was certainly courteous and kind.

Lafayette joined the war in 1777 and soon became close to Washington. They remained good friends throughout Washington's lifetime.

Washington loved dogs and had packs of foxhounds. Some were pets and are mentioned by name in his diaries.

> General Washington's compliments to General Howe. He does himself the pleasure to return him a dog, which accidentally fell into his hands, and by the inscription on the Collar, appears to belong to General Howe.

TO MARQUIS DE LAFAYETTE, DECEMBER 31, 1777 (EXCERPT)
From Headquarters

Washington's leadership was questioned in late 1777. Some members of Congress and officers of the army felt that Horatio Gates, who had just won a major victory at the Battle of Saratoga in New York, was more capable.

(Gates thought so, too!) Washington, on the other hand, had just lost two major battles at Brandywine and Germantown in Pennsylvania, as well as the capital city of Philadelphia in September–October 1777. But even though he was criticized for his failures, Washington still had the support of the majority of Congress and the army.

Washington took seriously the attacks on his character and abilities.* He spent a good part of that winter dealing with his "enemies" and making sure his position was secured.

Throughout the war, Washington was clear about his position. He maintained a policy that the military was subordinate to civilian government and that as commander in chief he answered to Congress and the American people. He wrote to Henry Laurens, president of the Continental Congress, in early 1778, "My Enemies take an ungenerous advantage of me; they know the delicacy of my situation, and that motives of policy deprive me of the defence I might otherwise make against their insiduous attacks. They know I cannot combat their insinuations, however injurious, without disclosing secrets, it is of the utmost moment to conceal."

Washington depended on those loyal to him. France's Marquis de Lafayette, young and rich, had just joined the war in the summer of 1777. Lafayette admired Washington and came to think of him as a father. Washington treated Lafayette as the son he never had. The two remained loyal friends after the war.

> My Dear Marquis: Your favour of Yesterday conveyed to me fresh proof of that friendship and attachment which I have happily experienced since the first of our acquaintance, and for which I entertain sentiments of the purest affection. It will ever constitute part of my happiness to know that I stand well in your opinion, because I am satisfied that you can have no views to answer by throwing out false colours, and that you possess a Mind too exalted to condescend to dirty Arts and low intrigues to acquire a reputation. Happy, thrice happy, would it have been for this Army and the cause we are embarked in, if the same generous spirit had pervaded all the Actors in it. But one

---

*Washington believed a plot existed to give the command to Gates. Sometimes called the "Conway Cabal," it was reported to be headed by Samuel Adams, Richard Henry Lee, Thomas Mifflin, and Dr. Benjamin Rush. They supposedly used Inspector General Thomas Conway as the front man, in part to find out whether dissatisfaction with Washington was widespread among the people. Later, Horatio Gates became involved. There is still disagreement about whether or not the plot actually existed.

Gentleman, whose Name you have mentioned [Gates], had, I am confident, far different views. His ambition and great desire of being puffed off as one of the first Officers of the Age, could only be equalled by the means which he used to obtain them; but finding that I was determined not to go beyond the line of my duty to indulge him in the first, nor, to exceed the strictest rules of propriety, to gratify him in the second, he became my inveterate Enemy; and has, I am persuaded, practised every Art to do me an injury, even at the expense of reprobating a measure, which did not succeed, that he himself advised to. How far he may have accomplished his ends, I know not, and, but for considerations of a public Nature, I care not. For it is well known, that neither ambitious, nor lucrative motives led me to accept my present Appointments; in the discharge of which, I have endeavoured to observe one steady and uniform conduct, which I shall invariably pursue, while I have the honour to command, regardless of the Tongue of slander or the powers of detraction.

Washington and his troops spent the winter of 1777–1778 at Valley Forge, Pennsylvania.

TO JOHN BANISTER,* APRIL 21, 1778 (EXCERPT)
From Valley Forge

Desertion was high and morale low in the early months at Valley Forge. In April, however, the army was much better off. Food and clothing were

*Virginia delegate to Congress

more plentiful, and with the help of Baron von Steuben, the army was trained and much more disciplined.

Despite these improvements, however, Washington's officers were not satisfied and were resigning their commissions at an "alarming height." Some had gone home on furlough and did not want to return to army life. Congress was also in the process of reorganizing the army, and some of the officers were left without positions or refused to serve under less-experienced officers.

Washington continued to appeal to Congress for better conditions, particularly fair payment for his officers. He realized that men were motivated not just by a sense of patriotism but also by self-interest or the promise of good wages. If men did not benefit from the army in some way, Washington maintained that they would remain "without discipline, without energy, incapable of acting with vigor, and destitute of those cements necessary to promise success, on the one hand, or to withstand the shocks of adversity, on the other."

Besides the needs of his army, Washington addresses here the cause of independence and questions Britain's recent call for peace. Washington knew that America could survive only as an independent nation. He also knew then that his army—a stronger one based on his recommendation— could win the war only with the help of France. France was secretly providing the Patriots' cause with supplies at this time but would soon publicly enter the war.

> We must take the passions of Men as Nature has given them, and those principles as a guide which are generally the rule of Action. I do not mean to exclude altogether the Idea of Patriotism. I know it exists, and I know it has done much in the present Contest. But I will venture to assert, that a great and lasting War can never be supported on this principle alone. It must be aided by a prospect of Interest or some reward. For a time, it may, of itself push Men to Action; to bear much, to encounter difficulties; but it will not endure unassisted by Interest.
>
> The necessity of putting the Army upon a respectable footing, both as to numbers and constitution, is now become more essential than ever. The Enemy are beginning to play a Game more dangerous than their efforts by Arms, tho' these will not

Charles Willson Peale, who served in Pennsylvania's militia, painted portraits of many American officers during the war. Using bed ticking—a cloth covering—as a canvas, Peale was able to capture Washington's larger-than-life stature in this portrait from around 1780. Washington was over six feet tall and had long arms and legs and very large hands and feet. Washington is wearing a large hat with a ribboned ornament called a cockade and big epaulets on his shoulders.

be remitted in the smallest degree, and which threatens a fatal blow to American Independence, and to her liberties of course: They are endeavouring to ensnare the people by specious allurements of Peace. . . .

Whether we continue to War, or proceed to Negotiate, the Wisdom of America in Council cannot be too great. Our situation will be truly delicate. To enter into a Negotiation too hastily, or to reject it altogether, may be attended with consequences equally fatal. The wishes of the people, seldom founded in deep disquisitions, or resulting from other reasonings than their present feeling, may not intirely accord with our true policy and interest. If they do not, to observe a proper line of conduct, for promoting the one, and avoiding offence to the other, will be a Work of great difficulty. Nothing short of Independence, it appears to me, can possibly do. A Peace, on other terms, would, if I may be allowed the expression, be a Peace of War. The injuries we have received from the British Nation were so unprovoked; have been so great and so many, that they can never be forgotten. Besides the feuds, the jealousies; the animosities that would ever attend a Union with them. Besides the importance, the advantages we should derive from an unrestricted commerce; Our fidelity as a people; Our gratitude; Our Character as Men, are opposed to a coalition with them as subjects, but in case of the last extremity. Were we easily to accede to terms of dependence, no nation, upon future occasions, let the oppressions of Britain be never so flagrant and unjust, would interpose for our relief, or at least they would do it with a cautious reluctance and upon conditions, most probably, that would be hard, if not dishonourable to us. France, by her supplies, has saved us from the Yoke thus far, and a wise and virtuous perseverence, would and I trust will, free us entirely.

CIRCULAR TO THE NEW ENGLAND STATES, JANUARY 5, 1781
From Head Quarters, New Windsor

In early 1781, the Pennsylvania Line had had enough. Fed up with the lack of money, clothing, and food, and in dispute over their terms of enlistments, they mutinied at their camp near Morristown, New Jersey, where they were stationed. Determined to voice their grievances, the Pennsylvania men headed south to Philadelphia to let Congress and their state government know their demands. Washington, who was at headquarters in New Windsor, New York, understood his men's complaints. He had been reminding Congress about his troops' poor conditions ever since the war began.

For Washington the situation was critical. Without the authority of Congress, he first appealed to the states for money, clothing, and food.

Washington worried most about the effect the mutiny would have on the rest of his troops. Would this mutiny lead to others? And would the mutineers—tempted by the promise of money, clothing, food, pardons, and the possibility of leaving military service if they defected to the other side—join the British army?

Ultimately, the Pennsylvania troops did not join the British. Some who had fulfilled their enlistment requirements were discharged. Some were given time off. Many of the mutineers ended up reenlisting.

Washington was right about more revolts. A number of the New Jersey Brigade soon mutinied. Washington took immediate and deliberate action in order to put discipline back into the army. He not only stopped the mutineers from New Jersey but had two of their leaders executed.

Sir: It is with extreme anxiety, and pain of mind, I find myself constrained to inform Your Excellency that the event I have long apprehended would be the consequence of the complicated distresses of the Army, has at length taken place. On the night of the 1st instant a mutiny was excited by the Non Commissioned Officers and Privates of the Pennsylvania Line, which soon became so universal as to defy all opposition; in attempting to quell this tumult, in the first instance, some Officers were killed, others wounded, and the lives of several common Soldiers lost. Deaf to the arguments, entreaties, and utmost efforts of *all their Officers* to stop them, the Men moved off from Morris Town, the place of their Cantonment, with their Arms, and six pieces of Artillery: and from Accounts just received by Genl. Wayne's* Aid De Camp, they were still in a body, on their March to Philadelphia, to demand a redress of their grievances. At what point this defection will stop, or how extensive it may prove God only knows; at present the Troops at the important Posts in this vicinity remain quiet, not being acquainted with this unhappy and alarming affair; but how long they will continue so cannot be ascertained, as they labor under some of the pressing hardships, with the Troops who have revolted.

The aggravated calamities and distresses that have resulted, from the total want of pay for nearly twelve Months, for want of cloathing, at a severe season, and not unfrequently the want of provisions; are beyond description. The circumstances will now point out much more forcibly what ought to be done, than any thing that can possibly be said by me, on the subject.

It is not within the sphere of my duty to make requisitions, without the Authority of Congress, from individual States: but at such a crisis, and circumstanced as we are, my own heart will acquit me; and Congress, and the States (eastward of this) whom for the sake of dispatch, I address, I am persuaded will excuse me, when once for all I give it decidedly as my opinion,

---

*Anthony Wayne was in charge of putting down the mutiny.

that it is in vain to think an Army can be kept together much longer, under such a variety of sufferings as ours has experienced: and that unless some immediate and spirited measures are adopted to furnish at least three Months pay to the Troops, in Money that will be of some value to them; And at the same time ways and means are devised to cloath and feed them better (more regularly I mean) than they have been, the worst that can befall us may be expected.

I have transmitted Congress a Copy of this Letter, and have in the most pressing manner requested them to adopt the measure which I have above recommended, or something similar to it, and as I will not doubt of their compliance, I have thought proper to give you this previous notice, that you may be prepared to answer the requisition.

As I have used every endeavour in my power to avert the evil that has come upon us, so will I continue to exert every means I am possessed of to prevent an extension of the Mischief, but I can neither foretell, or be answerable for the issue.

That you may have every information that an officer of rank and abilities can give of the true situation of our affairs, and the condition and temper of the Troops I have prevailed upon Brigadier Genl Knox to be the bearer of this Letter, to him I beg leave to refer your Excellency for many Matters which would be too tedious for a Letter. I have the honor etc.

TO DOCTOR JOHN BAKER, MAY 29, 1781
From New Windsor

Throughout his life, Washington's real and false teeth caused him problems and much discomfort. He started losing his teeth in his twenties and by the time he was president had only one real tooth left. Washington's false teeth were constantly wearing out, coming loose, or forcing his lips to protrude. They also tended to turn black from the port wine he drank or soaked them in. Washington was advised to soak his teeth in clean water and then rub them with chalk and a pine or cedar stick to keep them white. If he preferred his teeth yellow he was told to soak them in "Broath or pot liquer."

Sir: A day or two ago I requested Colo. Harrison to apply to you for a pair of Pincers to fasten the wire of my teeth. I hope you furnished him with them. I now wish you would send me one of your scrapers, as my teeth stand in need of cleaning, and I have little prospect of being in Philadelpa. soon. It will come very safe by the Post, and in Return, the money shall be sent so soon as I know the cost of it. I am, etc.

Cornwallis was too ill to come to the surrender ceremony at Yorktown on October 19, 1781. Instead, he sent his second in command, Brigadier General Charles O'Hara, to deliver his sword. Not to be outdone, Washington (on the white horse) did not receive the sword but allowed General Benjamin Lincoln, his second in command, to accept it. Lincoln had suffered a defeat to the British at Charleston in 1780.

TO THE PRESIDENT OF CONGRESS, OCTOBER 19, 1781
From Head Quarters near York

The Yorktown campaign was Washington's greatest victory and the event that caused the British to eventually pack up and go home. Washington was able to defeat Britain's General Lord Cornwallis with the support and help of the French army, under the leadership of General Rochambeau, and the French navy, under the command of Admiral de Grasse. Cornwallis requested a cease fire on October 17, 1781, to negotiate surrender terms for his army. Two days later, his forces formally surrendered.

Sir: I have the Honor to inform Congress, that a Reduction of the British Army under the Command of Lord Cornwallis, is most happily effected. The unremitting Ardor which actuated every Officer and Soldier in the combined Army on this Occasion, has principally led to this Important Event, at an earlier period than my most sanguine Hopes had induced me to expect.

The singular Spirit of Emulation, which animated the whole Army from the first Commencement of our Operations, has filled my Mind with the highest pleasure and Satisfaction, and had given me the happiest presages of Success.

On the 17th instant, a Letter was received from Lord Cornwallis, proposing a Meeting of Commissioners, to consult on Terms for the Surrender of the Posts of York and Gloucester. This Letter (the first which had passed between us) opened a Correspondence, a Copy of which I do myself the Honor to inclose; that Correspondence was followed by the Definitive Capitulation, which was agreed to, and Signed on the 19th. Copy of which is also herewith transmitted, and which I hope, will meet the Approbation of Congress.

I should be wanting in the feelings of Gratitude, did I not mention on this Occasion, with the warmest Sense of Acknowledgements, the very chearfull and able Assistance, which I have received in the Course of our Operations, from his Excellency the Count de Rochambeau, and all his Officers of every Rank, in their respective Capacities. Nothing could equal this Zeal of our Allies, but the emulating Spirit of the American Officers, whose Ardor would not suffer their Exertions to be exceeded.

The very uncommon Degree of Duty and Fatigue which the Nature of the Service required from the Officers of Engineers and Artillery of both Armies, obliges me particularly to mention the Obligations I am under to the Commanding and other Officers of those Corps.

I wish it was in my Power to express to Congress, how much I feel myself indebted to The Count de Grasse and the Officers of the Fleet under his Command for the distinguished Aid and Support which have been afforded by them; between whom, and the Army, the most happy Concurrence of Sentiments and

Views have subsisted, and from whom, every possible Cooperation has been experienced, which the most harmonious Intercourse could afford.

Returns of the Prisoners, Military Stores, Ordnance Shipping and other Matters, I shall do myself the Honor to transmit to Congress as soon as they can be collected by the Heads of Departments, to which they belong.

Colo. Laurens and the Viscount de Noiailles, on the Part of the combined Army, were the Gentlemen who acted as Commissioners for formg and settg the Terms of Capitulation and Surrender herewith transmitted, to whom I am particularly obliged for their Readiness and Attention exhibited on the Occasion.

Colo Tilghman, one of my Aids de Camp, will have the Honor to deliver these Dispatches to your Excellency; he will be able to inform you of every minute Circumstance which is not particularly mentioned in my Letter; his Merits, which are too well known to need my observations at this time, have gained my particular Attention, and could wish that they may be [h]onored with the Notice of your Excellency and Congress.

Your Excellency and Congress will be pleased to accept my Congratulations on this happy Event, and believe me to be With the highest Respect etc.

P. S. Tho' I am not possessed of the Particular Returns, yet I have reason to suppose that the Number of Prisoners will be between five and Six thousand, exclusive of Seamen and others.

TO MARQUIS DE LAFAYETTE, NOVEMBER 15, 1781 (EXCERPT)
From Mount Vernon in Virginia

Yorktown did not mark the end of the fighting. Immediately after his victory there, Washington wanted to push farther south to the Carolinas and Georgia to meet the British positioned there, but the French fleet had obligations in the West Indies and could not help out. Washington believed that the end of the war would come only with the support of the superior French fleet.

One month after Yorktown, in a letter to his French friend, Washington discusses his next campaign, hoping that the French fleet will return the following May and resume her role in the Patriot cause. (It never did return.)

In the meantime, Washington and his troops headed back to New York to monitor the action of the British army stationed there. Little did Washington know that the fighting was, for the most part, over. The war was unpopular in England and had caused severe financial problems—a high national debt and taxes. Two years later, the war would officially end with the signing of the Treaty of Paris.

As you expressed a desire to know my Sentiments respecting the operations of next Campaign before your departure for France I will, without a tedious display of reasoning, declare in one word, that the advantages of it to America, and the honor and glory of it to the Allied Arms in these States, must depend *absolutely* upon the Naval force which is employed in these Seas, and the time of its appearance next year. No land force can act decisively unless it is accompanied by a Maritime superiority; nor can more than negative advantages be expected without it; for proof of this, we have only to recur to the instances of the ease and facility with which the British shifted their ground as advantages were to be obtained at either extremity of the Continent, and to their late heavy loss the moment they failed in their Naval Superiority. To point out the further advantages which might have been obtained in the course of this year if Count de Grasse could have waited, and would have covered a further operation to the Southward, is unnecessary; because a doubt did not, nor does at this moment remain upon any Mans Mind of the total extirpation of the British force in the Carolina's and Georgia, if he could have extended his co-operation two Months longer.

It follows then as certain as that night succeeds the day, that without a decisive Naval force we can do nothing definitive. and with it, every thing honourable and glorious. A constant Naval superiority would terminate the War speedily; without it, I do not know that it will ever be terminated honourably. If this force should appear early, we shall have the whole Campaign before us. The Months of June to September Inclusive, are well adapted for operating in any of the States to the Northward of this; and the remaining Months are equally well suited to those South of it: in which time, with such means, I think much, I will add, every thing, might be expected.

CIRCULAR TO THE STATES, JUNE 8, 1783 (EXCERPTS)
From Head Quarters, Newburgh

By the middle of March, Washington knew that the war between Great Britain and the United States had formally ended. On April 19, the anniversary of the battles of Lexington and Concord, he ordered that the end of hostilities between the two countries be "publickly proclaimed." Now all he had to do was wait until the end of the war was officially recognized by the participating governments.

Washington had lots to do before then—discharge troops, promote fair pay for his men, and orchestrate an exchange of prisoners. He also needed to write his farewell to the public.

Washington conveys his thoughts about the future of the country to the people who needed the most convincing, the governors of the states. The states needed to come together to form a strong central government, and Washington urges each governor to "communicate these sentiments to your Legislature."

Besides unity, the letter addresses the war's debts, troop reimbursements, a strong defense, and the role of Congress. Washington also takes the time to submit his resignation from public office. He writes, "I bid a last farewell to the cares of Office, and all the imployments of public life." His retirement lasted about four years, until he attended the Constitutional Convention from May to September 1787.

This document is considered by many historians to be one of Washington's most important works. He considered it his "legacy." Highly praised, the letter was reprinted in newspapers and as a separate publication and was referred to and studied for many years.

There are four things, which I humbly conceive, are essential to the well being, I may even venture to say, to the existence of the United States as an Independent Power:

1st. An indissoluble Union of the States under one Federal Head.

2dly. A Sacred regard to Public Justice.

3dly. The adoption of a proper Peace Establishment, and

4thly. The prevalence of that pacific and friendly Disposition, among the People of the United States, which will induce them to forget their local prejudices and policies, to make those mutual concessions which are requisite to the general prosperity, and in some instances, to sacrifice their individual advantages to the interest of the Community.

These are the Pillars on which the glorious Fabrick of our Independency and National Character must be supported; Liberty is the Basis, and whoever would dare to sap the foundation, or overturn the Structure, under whatever specious pretexts he may attempt it, will merit the bitterest execration, and the severest punishment which can be inflicted by his injured Country.

The circular's last paragraph is poetic.

I now make it my earnest prayer, that God would have you, and the State over which you preside, in his holy protection, that he would incline the hearts of the Citizens to cultivate a spirit of subordination and obedience to Government, to entertain a brotherly affection and love for one another, for their fellow Citizens of the United States at large, and particularly for their brethren who have served in the Field, and finally, that he would most graciously be pleased to dispose us all, to do Justice, to love mercy, and to demean ourselves with that Charity, humility and pacific temper of mind, which were the Characteristicks of the Divine Author of our blessed Religion, and without an humble imitation of whose example in these things, we can never hope to be a happy Nation.

Rockingham (top), a farm in Rocky Hill, New Jersey, was Washington's last headquarters during the Revolutionary War. He lived there from August to November of 1783 and attended congressional meetings at Nassau Hall (bottom) in nearby Princeton, the nation's capital. Today Rockingham is a state historic site located in Franklin Township, and Nassau Hall is still a part of Princeton University.

FAREWELL ORDERS TO THE ARMIES OF THE UNITED STATES, NOVEMBER 2, 1783 (EXCERPT)
From Rock[y] Hill, near Princeton

In late August 1783, Washington was anxious for the war to officially end, and he was eager to return to Mount Vernon. He was living in New Jersey at Rockingham, a country farm in Rocky Hill, and attending congressional meetings in nearby Princeton. Washington remained at Rockingham, his last wartime headquarters, for three months. It was here he learned that the Treaty of Paris had been signed. Washington would finally return to his beloved Mount Vernon by Christmas Eve, 1783.

At Rockingham, Washington wrote his farewell orders to his troops, referring to himself in the third person. Washington calls his troops a "disciplined Army form'd at once from such raw materials," "one patriotic band of Brothers," and thanks them for "the assistance he has received from every Class, and in every instance." Washington promises his troops bright futures, well-earned compensation ("which must and will most inevitably be paid"), and an easy transition to civilian life if they carry with them "conciliating dispositions." Washington's ending is personal and sentimental, almost fatherly.

> He presents his thanks in the most serious and affectionate manner to the General Officers, as well for their counsel on many interesting occasions, as for their Order in promoting the success of the plans he had adopted. To the Commandants of Regiments and Corps, and to the other Officers for their great zeal and attention, in carrying his orders promptly into execution. To the Staff, for their alacrity and exactness in performing the Duties of their several Departments. And to the Non Commissioned Officers and private Soldiers, for their extraordinary patience in suffering, as well as their invincible fortitude in Action. To the various branches of the Army the General takes this last and solemn opportunity of professing his inviolable attachment and friendship. He wishes more than bare professions were in his power, that he were really able to be useful to them all in future life. He flatters himself however, they will do him the justice to believe, that whatever could with

propriety be attempted by him has been done, and being now to conclude these his last public Orders, to take his ultimate leave in a short time of the military character, and to bid a final adieu to the Armies he has so long had the honor to Command, he can only again offer in their behalf his recommendations to their grateful country, and his prayers to the God of Armies. May ample justice be done them here, and may the choicest of heaven's favours, both here and hereafter, attend those who, under the devine auspices, have secured innumerable blessings for others; with these wishes, and this benediction, the Commander in Chief is about to retire from Service. The Curtain of seperation will soon be drawn, and the military scene to him will be closed for ever.

A month after writing these orders, Washington said farewell to his officers at Fraunces Tavern in New York City, personally thanking each one. The scene was said to be so emotional that Washington and many of his officers wept.

Washington said good-bye to his officers on December 4, 1783, at Fraunces Tavern in New York City. The nineteenth-century oil painting *G. Washington's Farewell Interview with the Generals of his Army on Retiring from his Command* captures that moment. The oil painting is attributed to American artist Christopher Lawrence, who lived from 1792 to 1879.

CHAPTER FIVE

FARMER, LANDOWNER, AND POLITICIAN

TO LAFAYETTE, FEBRUARY 1, 1784 (EXCERPT)
From Mount Vernon

WASHINGTON RETURNED TO MOUNT VERNON "an older man by near nine years." Although he looked forward to retirement, he had much to do. At the end of this letter Washington responds to Lafayette's invitation to visit France: "At present I see but little prospect of such a voyage, the deranged situation of my private concerns, occasioned by an absence of almost nine years, and an entire disregard of all private business during that period, will not only suspend, but may put it forever out of my power to gratify this wish."

But if Washington feels worried about the state of his affairs, he also feels satisfied being back home. He captures these peaceful feelings beautifully in the letter's opening paragraph.

> At length my Dear Marquis I am become a private citizen on the banks of the Potomac, & under the shadow of my own Vine & my own Fig tree, free from the bustle of a camp & the busy scenes of public life, I am solacing myself with those tranquil enjoyments, of which the Soldier who is ever in pursuit of

fame—the Statesman whose watchful days & sleepless Nights are spent in devising schemes to promote the welfare of his own—perhaps the ruin of other countries, as if this Globe was insufficient for us all—& the Courtier who is always watching the countenance of his Prince, in hopes of catching a gracious smile, can have very little conception. I am not only retired from all public employments, but I am retireing within myself; & shall be able to view the solitary walk, & tread the paths of private life with heartfelt satisfaction—Envious of none, I am determined to be pleased with all. & this my dear friend, being the order for my march, I will move gently down the stream of life, until I sleep with my Fathers.

TO LAFAYETTE, DECEMBER 8, 1784 (EXCERPT)
From Mount Vernon

In retirement, Washington thought of death, which is surprising since he had just spent eight years fighting a war. But at the age of fifty-two, Washington had lived longer than most of the men in his family. His grandfather had died at thirty-eight, his father at forty-nine, his half brothers Lawrence and Augustine at thirty-four and forty-two respectively, and his brother Sam at forty-seven. Washington would outlive his remaining two brothers, John Augustine and Charles, and his sister, Betty. Washington's mother would live the longest of them all, dying of breast cancer in her early eighties.

I called to mind the days of my youth, & found they had long since fled to return no more; that I was now descending the hill, I had been 52 years climbing—& that tho' I was blessed with a good constitution, I was of a short lived family—and might soon expect to be entombed in the dreary mansions of my father's—These things darkened the shades & gave a gloom to the picture, consequently to my prospects of seeing you again: but I will not repine—I have had my day.

Robert Edge Pine was a successful British painter who moved to the United States in the mid-1780s. In 1785, Pine traveled to Mount Vernon to paint Washington's portrait, finishing it two years later in Philadelphia. Three versions of this portrait exist (at Smithsonian's National Portrait Gallery, at Independence National Historical Park [shown here], and in the Warner Collection of Gulf States Paper Corporation, Tuscaloosa, Alabama).
Washington was in his early fifties and would soon be the country's first president. Other family members also were painted by Pine in 1785.

TO ROBERT MORRIS, APRIL 12, 1786 (EXCERPT)
From Mount Vernon

Slavery was a way of life for the people of Virginia and the rest of the South. Although Washington was a slaveholder for all of his adult life, he became troubled by the institution after the war, probably stimulated by the revolutionary literature of the time.

Even though Washington did not sell any of his slaves and purchased only a few starting in the late 1700s, his slave population grew as the slaves' families became larger.

Slaves at Mount Vernon were treated fairly well and felt free to complain when they weren't. Washington was one of the few planters who provided for the freeing of his own slaves after his death.

Although he seemed to be privately opposed to slavery, Washington did nothing to end it in his public roles as a burgessman, member of the Continental Congress, or president. He never publicly spoke out against the institution, largely because of the destructive effect such a controversy would have on the fragile young republic.

In this letter to Robert Morris, a financier, Washington takes a stand against the Society of Quakers in Philadelphia, which was attempting to liberate a slave visiting the city with his master. (The slave's owner was being sued by the society.) Washington felt that the actions of the Quakers were unlawful and believed that the only way to abolish slavery was through legislation, not through the efforts of individuals or private societies.

I hope it will not be conceived from these observations, that it is my wish to hold the unhappy people who are the subject of this letter, in slavery. I can only say that there is not a man living who wishes more sincerely than I do, to see a plan adopted for the abolition of it—but there is only one proper and effectual mode by which it can be accomplished, & that is by Legislative authority: and this, as far as my suffrage will go, shall never be wanting.

But when slaves who are happy & content to remain with their present masters, are tampered with & seduced to leave them; when masters are taken at unawar[e]s by these practices; when a conduct of this sort begets discontent on one side and resentment on the other, & when it happens to fall on a man whose purse will not measure with that of the Society, & he looses his property for want of means to defend it—it is oppression in the latter case, & not humanity in any; because it introduces more evils than it can cure.

TO JOHN JAY, MAY 18, 1786 (EXCERPT)
From Mount Vernon

About a year before the Constitutional Convention met, Washington wrote Secretary of Foreign Affairs John Jay about the weaknesses of the present government and the unfortunate state of the country. Under the leadership of Daniel Shays, a group of farmers in Massachusetts would soon lead a revolt against high taxes and their state's financial policies. And four months later, a convention would meet in Annapolis to address commercial concerns between the states and to propose the need for a national convention to revise the Articles of Confederation, the framework under which the government was currently operating.

For many years, Washington argued for a central government rather than a loose confederation of states. Although here he supports changes to the Articles, he is not convinced that people are able to make the right decisions at this time.

Throughout 1786 and 1787, Washington grew to respect the opinions of fellow Virginian James Madison, who was then working on an alternative to the Articles. Madison would become perhaps the most important delegate at the Constitutional Convention. He is known as the Father of the Constitution.

> I coincide perfectly in sentiment with you, my dear Sir, that there are errors in our National Government which call for correction; loudly I will add; but I shall find my self happily mistaken if the remedies are at hand. We are certainly in a delicate situation, but my fear is that the people are not yet sufficiently misled to retract from error! To be plainer, I think there is more wickedness than ignorance, mixed with our councils. Under this impression, I scarcely know what opinion to entertain of a general Convention. That it is necessary to revise, and amend the articles of Confederation, I entertain *no* doubt; but what may be the consequences of such an attempt *is* doubtful. Yet, something must be done, or the fabrick must fall. It certainly is tottering! Ignorance & design, are difficult to combat. Out of these proceed illiberality, *improper* jealousies, and a train of evils which oftentimes, in republican governments, must be sorely felt before they can be removed. The former, that is ignorance, being a fit soil for the latter to work in, tools are employed which a generous mind would disdain to use; and which nothing but time, and their own puerile or wicked productions, can show the inefficacy and dangerous tendency of. I think often of our situation, and view it with concern. From the high ground on which we stood— from the plain path which invited our footsteps, to be so fallen!—so lost! is really mortifying. But virtue, I fear, has, in a great degree, taken its departure from our Land, and the want of disposition to do justice is the sourse of the national embarrassments; for under whatever guise or colourings are given to them, this, I apprehend, is the origin of the evils we now feel, & probably shall labour for sometime yet.

Independence Hall in Philadelphia, Pennsylvania, was first known as the Pennsylvania State House. Inside is the room where the Constitution and the Declaration of Independence were discussed and signed and where Washington received the command of the Continental army. The chair that Washington used when he was president of the Constitutional Convention (rear of top right photograph) is still in the room today (see also page 70).

TO JAMES MADISON, MARCH 31, 1787 (EXCERPT)
From Mount Vernon

Three days before writing to Madison, Washington had written to Edmund Randolph, Virginia's governor, and agreed to attend the Constitutional Convention in Philadelphia, health permitting.

Washington had at first declined. He worried about coming out of retirement, "appearing on a public theatre after a public declaration to the contrary." He worried about offending the Society of the Cincinnati, a group of former Revolutionary War officers.* (Washington had already declined an invitation to attend its meeting in Philadelphia, which was to take place at the same time as the Constitutional Convention.) He worried about the legality of a meeting to amend the Articles. And he worried about his health. He wrote Randolph, "I have, of late, been so much afflicted with a rheumatic complaint in my shoulder that at times I am hardly able to raise my hand to my head, or turn myself in bed."

Washington knew that his indecisiveness and his health might cause Randolph to find a replacement. This is probably why he doesn't mention attending the convention to Madison. At that point, he wasn't sure if he was going.

> It gives me pleasure to hear that there is a probability of a full Representation of the States in Convention; but if the delegates come to it under fetters, the salutary ends proposed will in my opinion be greatly embarrassed & retarded, if not altogether defeated. I am anxious to know how this matter really is, as my wish is, that the Convention may adopt no temporising expedient, but probe the defects of the Constitution to the bottom, and provide radical cures, whether they are agreed to or not—a conduct like this, will stamp wisdom and dignity on the proceedings, and be looked to as a luminary, which sooner or later will shed its influence.

---

*Washington had been president general of the society since its beginning in 1783. In 1786 he considered stepping down, partly because of concerns over the widespread opposition to the society that had arisen during the early 1780s. The society's meetings took place during the convention, but Washington did not attend any of them (although he did go to dinner with the members on May 15). He retained his position as president general until his death, but his role became increasingly ceremonial. In 1784 Washington had proposed changing some of the rules that critics had found most objectionable (membership being passed down through eldest sons, for example), but the amendments to the society's institution were never ratified by the various state branches.

At the close of the Constitutional Convention, Benjamin Franklin declared that the sun on the back of Washington's chair was rising rather than setting. (He had been thinking about this throughout the convention.) Franklin was optimistic about what had taken place and the future of the country.

Henry Hintermeister (1897–1970) painted *Washington Directs the Signing of the Constitution* in oil in 1925.

TO BUSHROD WASHINGTON, NOVEMBER 9, 1787 (EXCERPTS)
From Mount Vernon

Washington quietly worked to have the Constitution ratified in Virginia. Many historians feel that he did not speak out on the subject for one important reason. Washington knew that he had a good chance of becoming president, and he may have felt that taking a public role could make him appear self-serving.

In this letter to his nephew, Washington promotes the power of the Constitution and addresses its opponents. For him, the point of dispute lies in the question "Is it best for the States to unite [proponents], or not to unite [opponents]?" In other words, the Constitution should not serve one state or a minority of states, but "the Union of the whole is a desirable object." Washington calls for the parts—states—to yield a little to bring about this union. In the following excerpt, he warns of what will happen to Virginia if it fails to vote for ratification.

Seven months later, on June 25, 1788, Virginia ratified the Constitution.

But to sum up the whole, let the opponants of the proposed Constitution, *in this State,* be asked—it is a question they ought certainly to have asked themselves; What line of conduct they would advise it to adopt, if nine other States should accede to it, of which I think there is little doubt? Would they recommend that it should stand on its own basis—seperate & distinct from the rest? Or would they connect it with Rhode Island, or even say two others, checkerwise, & remain with them as outcasts from the Society, to shift for themselves? or will they advise a return to our former dependence on Great Britain for their protection & support? or lastly would they prefer the mortification of comg in, when they will have no credit there from? I am sorry to add in this place that Virginians entertain *too* high an opinion of the importance of their own Country. In extent of territory—In number of Inhabitants *(of all descriptions)* & In wealth I will readily grant that it certainly stands first in the Union; but in point of *strength,* it is, comparitively, weak. To this point, my opportunities authorise me to speak, decidedly; and sure I am, in every point of view, in which the subject can be placed, it is not (considering also the Geographical situation of the State) more the interest of any one of them to confederate, than it is the one in which we live.

Washington knows that the Constitution is not "free from imperfections" but realizes that its real power would "always be with the people," who will interpret it according to their needs. "It is entrusted for certain defined purposes and for a certain limited period to representatives of their own chusing; and whenever it is exercised contrary to their interests, or not according to their wishes, their Servants can, and undoubtedly will be, recalled."

Washington ends his letter with advice about political life. Bushrod Washington had recently been elected to the Virginia legislature and would later attend the ratifying convention. Washington strictly followed his own advice. He rarely spoke out and earned the reputation as a patient and intelligent observer and listener.

> one piece of advice only I will give you on the occasion (if you mean to be a respectable member, and to entitle yourself to the Ear of the House)—and that is—except in local matters which respect your Constituents and to which you are obliged, by duty, to speak, rise but seldom—let this be on important matters—and then make yourself thoroughly acquainted with the subject. Never be agitated by *more than* a decent *warmth*, & offer your sentiments with modest diffidence—opinions thus given, are listened to with more attention than when delivered in a dictatorial stile. The latter, if attended to at all, altho they may *force* conviction, is sure to convey disgust also.

To Alexander Spotswood, February 13, 1788 (Excerpt)
From Mount Vernon

Washington truly loved being a farmer. These three sentences to his friend, a fellow farmer and Revolutionary War officer, reveal how difficult it must have been for him to come out of retirement a little over a year later and leave Mount Vernon.

> I think with you that the life of a Husbandman of all others, is the most delectable. It is honorable—It is amusing—and with Judicious management, it is profitable. To see plants rise from the Earth and flourish by the superior skill, and bounty of the labouror fills a contemplative mind with ideas which are more easy to be conceived than expressed.

Washington was happiest at Mount Vernon, tending to his fields, farms, workers, and family. His home appears in the background. This color lithograph was published in Paris around 1853.

To Henry Lee, Jr.,* September 22, 1788 (excerpt)
From Mount Vernon

By late 1787, almost everyone wanted Washington to be president. Newspapers called him the president-to-be and friends urged him to accept when the time came. The July 4 celebrations in 1788 were an outcry for his election.

Washington seemed to thrive on the fact that he was needed, that people came to him for leadership. But this was a tough decision. To accept would mean great risks to his reputation (he had publicly retired from office five years earlier) and to his health, and also giving up the quiet and good life at Mount Vernon. He knew he could not refuse the position before it was offered—it would seem as if he did not recognize the greatness of the job. The only way he could refuse it was if a more humble, available, and capable candidate were to be offered the position instead.

Washington never wanted to appear too bold or too proud. As he did

---

*Henry Lee, Jr., "Light Horse Harry" Lee, was a Revolutionary War hero and friend of Washington.

when he accepted the command of the Continental forces, he also was not totally confident he could manage the job. In his address to Charles Thomson (see pages 77–78) when he accepts the position as president of the country, Washington points to his inabilities. Perhaps he is also worried that if he fails as president his reputation will be permanently ruined.

> If I declined the task it would be upon quite another principle. Notwithstanding my advanced season of life, my encreasing fondness for Agricultural amusements, and my growing love of retirement augment and confirm my decided predeliction for the character of a private Citizen: Yet it would be no one of these motives, nor the hazard to which my former reputation might be exposed, or the terror of encountering new fatigues & troubles that would deter me from an acceptance—but a belief that some other person, who had less pretence & less inclination to be excused, could execute all the duties full as satisfactorily as myself. To say more would be indiscreet; as a disclosure of a refusal beforehand, might incur the application of the Fable, in which the Fox is represented as undervaluing the Grapes he could not reach. You will perceive, my dear Sir, by what is here observed (and which you will be pleased to consider in the light of a confidential communication) that my inclinations will dispose & decide me to remain as I am; unless a clear & insurmountable conviction should be impressed on my mind, that some very disagreeable consequences must in all human probability result from the indulgence of my wishes.

TO GEORGE STEPTOE WASHINGTON, MARCH 23, 1789 (EXCERPT)
From Mount Vernon

Washington's nephews George Steptoe and his brother Lawrence Augustine were always getting into trouble, causing Washington much distress. (Washington helped with his nephews' housing, schooling, and clothing.)

Washington had definite ideas about the qualities of a proper gentleman. In this letter, he outlines the characteristics necessary for a young man to take on and warns his nephew that if he behaves "in such a manner as to occasion any complaints being made to me—you may depend upon losing that place which you now have in my affections—and any future hopes you may have from me." But, on the other hand, if his conduct should merit Washington's regard, his nephew may "always depend upon the warmest attachment" from his affectionate friend and uncle.

At this time Washington was worried more than ever about his own reputation. George and Lawrence were about to go live with Washington's close friends Dr. and Mrs. James Craik, and Washington knew that he would soon become the country's president. Washington had no time for any embarrassing relatives.

> You have now arrived to that age when you must quit the trifling amusements of a boy, and assume the more dignified manners of a man. At this crisis your conduct will attract the notice of those who are about you; and as the first impressions are generally the most lasting, your doings now may mark the leading traits of your Character through life. It is therefore, absolutely necessary, if you mean to make any figure upon the Stage, that you should take the first steps right. What these steps are—and what general line is to be pursued to lay the foundation of an honorable and happy progress, is the part of age and experience to point out. This I shall do, as far as is in my power, with the utmost chearfulness; and I trust, that your own good sense will shew you the necessity of following it.
>
> The first and great object with you at present is to acquire, by industry and application, such knowledge as your situation enables you to obtain, and as will be useful to you in life. In doing this two other important objects will be gained besides the acquisition of knowledge—namely, a habit of industry, and a disrelish of that profusion of money & dissipation of time which are ever attendant upon idleness. I do not mean by a close application to your Studies that you should never enter into those amusements which are suited to your age and station. They may be made to go hand in hand with each other— and, used in their proper seasons, will ever be found to be a mutual assistance to each other. But what amusements are to be taken, and when, is the great matter to be attended to. Your

own judgement, with the advice of your *real* friends who may have an opportunity of a personal intercourse with you can point out the particular manner in which you may best spend your moments of relaxation, much better than I can at a distance. One thing, however, I would strongly impress upon you, viz., that when you have leisure to go into Company that it should always be of the best kind that the place you are in will afford; by this means you will be constantly improving your manners and cultivating your mind while you are relaxing from your books; and good Company will always be found much less expensive than bad. You cannot offer, as an excuse for not using it, that you cannot gain admission there—or that you have not a proper attention paid you in it; this is an apology made only by those whose manners are disgusting, or who<se character> is exceptionable; neither of which I hope, will ever be said of you.

CHAPTER SIX

THE COUNTRY'S FIRST PRESIDENT

The library (study) at Mount Vernon was photographed as it looked in the early twentieth century. In his will Washington gave his friend Dr. James Craik the tambour secretary (a desk with a rolling top) and chair shown at right. In the early 1900s, both pieces of furniture were returned to Mount Vernon.

Washington Receiving Notice of His Election by John Ward Dunsmore, oil on canvas, 1911. Compare this painting to the above photograph.

ADDRESS TO CHARLES THOMSON, APRIL 14, 1789

From Mount Vernon

WHEN CHARLES THOMSON, SECRETARY OF CONGRESS, arrived at Mount Vernon on April 14, 1789, carrying the official word of Washington's unanimous election as the country's first president, Washington was already aware of the news. He had started receiving reports about the election results as early as February and began to make plans to leave Mount Vernon. In fact, he had written this address days before.

Washington was well prepared to leave two days after Thomson's arrival. The trip to New York City, the country's temporary capital, was filled with stops at towns and cities along the way. Festivities were held in Alexandria, Baltimore, Philadelphia, Trenton, and New Brunswick. In Elizabeth Town, New Jersey, Washington stepped onto a barge that took him to New York City and to his new life as president.

Sir, I have been long accustomed to entertain so great a respect for the opinion of my fellow citizens, that the knowledge of their unanimous suffrages having been given in my favour scarcely leaves me the alternative for an Option. Whatever may have been my private feelings* and sentiments, I believe I cannot give a greater evidence of my sensibility for the honor they have done me than by accepting the appointment.

I am so much affected by this fresh proof of my country's esteem and confidence, that silence can best explain my gratitude—While I realize the arduous nature of the task which is conferred on me and feel my inability to perform it, I wish there may not be reason for regreting the choice. All I can promise is only that which can be accomplished by an honest zeal.

Upon considering how long time some of the gentlemen of both houses of Congress have been at New York, how anxiously desirous they must be to proceed to business and how deeply the public mind appears to be impressed with the necessity of doing it immediately I cannot find myself at liberty to delay my Journey—I shall therefore be in readiness to set out the day after to morrow, and shall be happy in the pleasure of your company. For you will permit me to say that it was a peculiar gratification to have received the communication from you.

FINAL VERSION OF FIRST INAUGURAL ADDRESS, NEW YORK, APRIL 30, 1789 (EXCERPT)

Some time before his inauguration, Washington had already given thought to what he wanted to say to members of Congress. A lengthy manuscript

---

*See pages 73–74.

was produced, probably by his secretary, David Humphreys, that Washington copied. Little is known about the differences between Humphreys's original draft (no copy has been found) and Washington's seventy-three-page copy. Apparently Washington copied the address to send to readers for advice but did not reveal who the author was. He, very wisely, had serious misgivings about its value—and certainly its length—as an address to Congress. Fragments of Washington's copy exist;* however, the final version that Washington delivered on April 30 bears no resemblance to it.

Perhaps remembering the conflicts that arose during the Constitution's ratification process, Washington now praises the members of the Senate and the House as fair and just and describes them as those who will come together to lay the foundations of a republican government. Washington refers to this enormous task as an experiment.

The title page of Benson J. Lossing's biography of George Washington features Washington taking the oath of office on April 30, 1789, at Federal Hall in New York City. On that day, Washington wore a suit of brown broadcloth woven in Hartford, Connecticut, and white silk stockings. Today a statue of George Washington by American sculptor John Quincy Adams Ward stands at this location.

"Undelivered First Inaugural Address: Fragments"

By the article establishing the Executive Department, it is made the duty of the President "to recommend to your consideration, such measures as he shall judge necessary and expedient." The circumstances under which I now meet you, will acquit me from entering into that subject, farther than to refer to the Great Constitutional Charter under which you are assembled; and which, in defining your powers, designates the objects to which your attention is to be given. It will be more consistent with those circumstances, and far more congenial with the feelings which actuate me, to substitute, in place of a recommendation of particular measures, the tribute that is due to the talents, the rectitude, and the patriotism which adorn the characters selected to devise and adopt them. In these honorable qualifications, I behold the surest pledges, that as on one side, no local prejudices, or attachments; no seperate views, nor party animosities, will misdirect the comprehensive and equal eye which ought to watch over this great Assemblage of communities and interests: so, on another, that the foundations of our national policy, will be laid in the pure and immutable principles of private morality; and the preeminence of free Government, be exemplified by all the attributes which can win the affections of its Citizens, and command the respect of the world. I dwell on this prospect with every satisfaction which an ardent love for my Country can inspire: since there is no truth more thoroughly established, than that there exists in the œconomy and course of nature, an indissoluble union between virtue and happiness, between duty and advantage, between the genuine maxims of an honest and magnanimous policy, and the solid rewards of public prosperity and felicity: Since we ought to be no less persuaded that the propitious smiles of Heaven, can never be expected on a nation that disregards the eternal rules of order and right, which Heaven itself has ordained: And since the preservation of the sacred fire of liberty, and the destiny of the Republican model of Government, are justly considered as *deeply*, perhaps as *finally* staked, on the experiment entrusted to the hands of the American people.

Washington and His First Cabinet by Thomas Prichard Rossiter (1818–1871). From left to right are Attorney General Edmund Randolph (in judicial robes), President Washington, Vice President John Adams (reading a document), Postmaster General Samuel Osgood (standing), Secretary of State Thomas Jefferson (seated in front), Secretary of War Henry Knox (quill in his mouth), and Secretary of the Treasury Alexander Hamilton. Technically, Adams and Osgood were not part of Washington's cabi-

To Thomas Jefferson, October 13, 1789 (Excerpt)

From New York

Washington selected men he knew and trusted to fill the heads of the great departments, later called the cabinet. Alexander Hamilton served as secretary of the treasury, Henry Knox as secretary of war, and Edmund Randolph as attorney general.

Jefferson was an ideal candidate for the position of secretary of state. He had served in the Virginia House of Burgesses and in the second and third Continental Congresses, as governor of Virginia, and most importantly, as minister to France. (The secretary of state's main duty is foreign relations.)

Jefferson was serving as minister to France in 1789. In October he sailed for home, intending to return to France. Washington's letter, however, greeted him in Virginia. Jefferson eventually accepted Washington's offer but soon grew disenchanted with the position. Political tensions divided the cabinet. Jefferson would serve during Washington's first term but would leave during his second term.

In the selection of characters to fill the important offices of Government in the United States I was naturally led to contemplate the talents and disposition which I knew you to possess and entertain for the Service of your Country. And without being able to consult your inclination, or to derive any knowledge of your intentions from your letters either to myself or to any other of your friends, I was determined, as well by motives of private regard as a conviction of public propriety, to nominate you for the Department of State, which under its present organization, involves many of the most interesting objects of the Executive Authority. But grateful as your acceptance of this Commission would be to me, I am at the sametime desirous to accommodate to your wishes, and I have therefore forborne to nominate your Successor at the Court of Versailles until I should be informed of your determination.

TO THE UNITED STATES SENATE AND HOUSE OF REPRESENTATIVES, JANUARY 8, 1790

Washington delivered annual addresses to the Senate and House, thus establishing a precedent that continues today with the president's State of the Union address. Washington's eight addresses mainly reviewed important issues of the past year and outlined plans for the future. The addresses dealt with such issues as the establishment of a more efficient and stable national military force; Indian affairs and the frontier; national finances; standardization of currency, weights, and measures; foreign affairs; neutrality; the Whiskey Rebellion; the establishment of the post office and post roads, the U.S. mint, a federal city, a national university, and a military academy; the manufacture of American goods; agriculture; commerce; and the promotion of science and literature. Washington, with the help of Congress, was creating a new working nation and establishing its position in the world.

Washington delivered his speech to Congress. It was later printed in several newspapers for everyone to read.

Fellow Citizens of the Senate, and House of Representatives.

I embrace with great satisfaction the opportunity, which now presents itself, of congratulating you on the present favourable prospects of our public affairs. The recent accession of the important State of North Carolina to the Constitution of the United States (of which official information has been received)—the rising credit and respectability of our Country—the general and increasing good will towards the Government of the Union—and the concord, peace and plenty, with which we are blessed, are circumstances, auspicious, in an eminent degree to our national prosperity.

In resuming your consultations for the general good, you cannot but derive encouragement from the reflection, that the measures of the last Session have been as satisfactory to your Constituents, as the novelty and difficulty of the work allowed you to hope. Still further to realize their expectations, and to secure the blessings which a Gracious Providence has placed within our reach, will in the course of the present important Session, call for the cool and deliberate exertion of your patriotism, firmness and wisdom.

Among the many interesting objects, which will engage your attention, that of providing for the common defence will merit particular regard. To be prepared for war is one of the most effectual means of preserving peace.

A free people ought not only to be armed but disciplined; to which end a Uniform and well digested plan is requisite: And their safety and interest require that they should promote such manufactories, as tend to render them independent on others, for essential, particularly for military supplies.

The proper establishment of the Troops which may be deemed indispensible, will be entitled to mature consideration. In the arrangements which may be made respecting it, it will be of importance to conciliate the comfortable support of the Officers and Soldiers with a due regard to œconomy.

There was reason to hope, that the pacific measures adopted with regard to certain hostile tribes of Indians would have relieved the inhabitants of our Southern and Western frontiers from their depredations. But you will percieve, from the information contained in the papers, which I shall direct to be laid before you (comprehending a communication from the Commonwealth of Virginia) that we ought to be prepared to afford protection to those parts of the Union; and, if necessary, to punish aggressors.

The interests of the United States require, that our intercourse with other nations should be facilitated by such provisions as will enable me to fulfil my duty in that respect, in the manner, which circumstances may render most conducive to the public good: And to this end, that the compensations to be made to the persons, who may be employed, should, according to the nature of their appointments, be defined by law; and a competent fund designated for defraying the expenses incident to the conduct of foreign affairs.

Various considerations also render it expedient, that the terms on which foreigners may be admitted to the rights of Citizens, should be speedily ascertained by a uniform rule of naturalization.

Uniformity in the Currency, Weights and Measures of the United States is an object of great importance, and will, I am persuaded, be duly attended to.

The advancement of Agriculture, commerce, and Manufactures, by all proper means, will not, I trust, need recommendation. But I cannot forbear intimating to you the expediency of giving effectual encouragement as well to the introduction of new and useful inventions from abroad, as to the exertions of skill and genius in producing them at home; and of facilitating the intercourse between the distant parts of our Country by a due attention to the Post-Office and Post Roads.

Nor am I less pursuaded, that you will agree with me in opinion, that there is nothing, which can better deserve your patrionage, than the promotion of Science and Literature. Knowledge is in every Country the surest basis of public happiness. In one, in which the measures of Government recieve their impression so immediately from the sense of the Community as in our's, it is proportionably essential. To the security of a free Constitution it contributes in various ways: By convincing those, who are entrusted with the public administration, that every valuable end of Government is best answered by the enlightened confidence of the people: And by teaching the people themselves to know and to value their own rights; to discern and provide against invasions of them; to distinguish between oppression and the necessary exercise of lawful authority; between burthens proceeding from a disregard to their convenience and those resulting from the inevitable exigencies of Society; to discriminate the spirit of liberty from that of licentiousness, cherishing the first, avoiding the last, and uniting a speedy, but temperate vigilence against encroachments, with an inviolable respect to the laws.

Whether this desirable object will be best promoted by affording aids to Seminaries of Learning already established—by the institution of a national University—or by any other expedients, will be well worthy of a place in the deliberations of the Legislature.

Gentlemen of the House of Representatives.

I saw with peculiar pleasure, at the close of the last Session, the resolution entered into by you expressive of your opinion, that an adequate provision for the support of the public Credit is a matter of high importance to the national honor and prosperity. In this sentiment, I entirely concur. And to a perfect confidence in your best endeavours to divise such a provision, as will be truly consistent with the end, I add an equal reliance on the chearful co-operation of the othe[r] branch of the Legislature. It would be superfluous to specify inducements to a measure in which the character and permanent interests of the United States are so obviously and so deeply concerned; and which has recieved so explicit a sanction from your declaration.

Gentlemen of the Senate and House of Representatives.

I have directed the proper Officers to lay before you respectively such papers and estimates as regard the affairs particularly recommended to your consideration, and necessary to convey to you that information of the state of the Union, which it is my duty to afford.

The welfare of our Country is the great object to which our cares and efforts ought to be directed. And I shall derive great satisfaction from a co-operation with you, in the pleasing though arduous task of ensuring to our fellow Citizens the blessings, which they have a right to expect, from a free, efficient and equal Government.

Go: Washington

TO ELIZABETH "BETTY" WASHINGTON LEWIS, OCTOBER 7, 1792 (EXCERPT)

From Mount Vernon

Harriot Washington was the daughter of Washington's brother Samuel and sister to George Steptoe and Lawrence Washington (see pages 74–76).

In the fall of 1792, Harriot went to live with her aunt Betty, Washington's sister. She had been living at Mount Vernon mostly under the care of Fanny Bassett, wife of Washington's nephew. (The Washingtons resided in New York City and Philadelphia from 1789 to 1797.) Like her unruly brothers, Harriot was in need of guidance and discipline. Washington looked to his sister to teach the teenager to pick up her clothes and to dress properly.

> Harriet [Harriot] has sense enough, but no disposition to industry, nor to be careful of her clothes. Your example and admonition, with proper restraints may overcome the two last; and to that end I wish you would examine her clothes and direct her in their use and application of them; for without this they will be, I am told, dabbed about in every hole and corner, and her best things always in use. Fanny was too easy, too much of her own indolent disposition and had too little authority to cause, either by precept or example, any change in this for the better and Mrs. Washington's absence has been injurious to her in many respects: but she is young, and with good advice may yet make a fine woman.

TO THE SECRETARY OF STATE (PRIVATE), OCTOBER 18, 1792

From Philadelphia

Thomas Jefferson and Alexander Hamilton did not get along. Jefferson favored a smaller government and more states' rights, while Hamilton favored a strong central government. Jefferson was drawn to the agricultural way of life of the South, while Hamilton endorsed the manufacturing city life of the North. Their differences paved the way for the two-party system. Jefferson was a Democratic-Republican, Hamilton a Federalist. Although Washington stayed away from party politics in the early years of his presidency, he later leaned more toward the Federalist Party.

My dear Sir: I did not require the evidence of the extracts which you enclosed me, to convince me of your attachment to the Constitution of the United States, or of your disposition to promote the general Welfare of this Country. But I regret, deeply regret, the difference in opinions which have arisen, and divided you and another principal Officer of the Government; and wish, devoutly, there could be an accommodation of them by mutual yieldings.

A Measure of this sort would produce harmony, and consequent good in our public Councils; the contrary will, inevitably, introduce confusion, and serious mischiefs; and for what? because mankind cannot think alike, but would adopt different means to attain the same end. For I will frankly, and solemnly declare that, I believe the views of both of you are pure, and well meant; and that experience alone will decide with respect to the salubrity of the measures wch. are the subjects of dispute. Why then, when some of the best Citizens in the United States, Men of discernment, Uniform and tried Patriots, who have no sinister views to promote, but are chaste in their ways of thinking and acting are to be found, some on one side, and some on the other of the questions which have caused these agitations, shd. either of you be so tenacious of your opinions as to make no allowances for those of the other? I could, and indeed was about to add more on this interesting subject; but will forbear, at least for the present; after expressing a wish that the cup wch. has been presented, may not be snatched from our lips by a discordance of *action* when I am persuaded there is no discordance in your *views*. I have a great, a sincere esteem and regard for you both, and ardently wish that some line could be marked out by which both of you could walk. I am &c.

PROCLAMATION OF NEUTRALITY, APRIL 22, 1793
From Philadelphia

When revolution broke out in France in 1789, Washington was beginning his first term of office. France's revolution, which brought about the downfall of the monarchy, affected its European neighbors, most noticeably Great Britain, and soon a full-fledged war was underway.

Since the United States was still bound by treaties negotiated with France during the Revolutionary War, Washington's neutral position concerning the European war created tensions at home. (Washington felt that the United States should concentrate on shaping its own country rather than on helping others to shape theirs.) The differences between the Democratic-Republicans and the Federalists became more pronounced. The Democratic-Republicans favored helping France, while the Federalists were pro-British.

Washington suffered politically and personally for his neutral position. Many people at the time sided with the Democratic-Republicans.

> Whereas it appears that a state of war exists between Austria, Prussia, Sardinia, Great Britain, and the United Netherlands, on the one part, and France on the other; and the duty and interest of the United States require, that they should with sincerity and good faith adopt and pursue a conduct friendly and impartial towards the belligerent powers:
>
> I have therefore thought fit by these presents, to declare the disposition of the United States to observe the conduct aforesaid towards those powers respectively; and to exhort and warn the citizens of the United States carefully to avoid all acts and proceedings whatsoever, which may in any manner tend to contravene such disposition.
>
> And I do hereby also make known, that whosoever of the citizens of the United States shall render himself liable to punishment or forfeiture under the law of nations, by committing, aiding or abetting hostilities against any of the said powers, or by carrying to any of them, those articles which are deemed contraband by the modern usage of nations, will not receive the protection of the United States against such punishment

or forfeiture; and further that I have given instructions to those officers to whom it belongs, to cause prosecutions to be instituted against all persons, who shall, within the cognizance of the Courts of the United States, violate the law of nations, with respect to the powers at war, or any of them.

To Thomas Jefferson, January 1, 1794
From Philadelphia

Washington wished that Hamilton and Jefferson could work out their differences and continue to serve him. Jefferson, however, resigned at the end of 1793, Hamilton in early 1795.

Dear Sir: I yesterday received, with sincere regret your resignation of the office of Secretary of State. Since it has been impossible to prevail upon you, to forego any longer the indulgence of your desire for private life; the event, however anxious I am to avert it, must be submitted to.

But I cannot suffer you to leave your Station, without assuring you, that the opinion, which I had formed, of your integrity and talents, and which dictated your original nomination, has been confirmed by the fullest experience; and that both have been eminently displayed in the discharge of your duties.

Let a conviction of my most earnest prayers for your happiness accompany you in your retirement; and while I accept with the warmest thanks your solicitude for my welfare, I beg you to believe that I always am &c.

This nineteenth-century engraving of the Washington family is based on Edward Savage's famous painting *The Washington Family,* done around 1796, and Savage's later engraving of the same painting. Pictured here are Washington, Martha, George Washington Parke Custis, Eleanor Parke Custis, and a slave at Mount Vernon, in uniform worn by house slaves and those attending the carriages.

This nineteenth-century lithograph is based on the same theme as the print on page 89, but the slave is no longer present, the positions of the Washington family have shifted, and the setting is drastically different—more in tune with the mid to late 1800s than the late 1700s.

TO ELIZABETH PARKE CUSTIS
SEPTEMBER 14, 1794 (EXCERPT)
From German Town, Pennsylvania

Washington and Martha were devoted grandparents to the four children of Martha's son, John Parke Custis, who died in 1781 at the age of 27. The youngest grandchildren, Eleanor "Nelly" Parke Custis and George Washington Parke Custis, lived with their grandparents. The eldest two, Elizabeth "Eliza" Parke Custis and Martha "Patsy" Parke Custis, lived with their mother, who had remarried two years after her husband's death.

Washington liked to offer advice to his grandchildren, his many nieces and nephews, and several children of friends. Eliza was only a teenager when Washington wrote her about love and marriage. Washington most likely considered his own marriage a good one. He and Martha got along well and supported one another. In 1794 they had been married for thirty-five years.

A year and a half later, Eliza married Thomas Law, a wealthy British businessman, but unfortunately the marriage was unhappy. Eliza and Thomas separated in 1804 and divorced in 1811.

Love is a mighty pretty thing; but like all other delicious things, it is cloying; and when the first transports of the passion begins to subside, which it assuredly will do, and yield—oftentimes too late—to more sober reflections, it serves to evince, that love is too dainty a food to live upon *alone,* and ought not to be considered farther than as a necessary ingredient for that matrimonial happiness which results from a combination of causes; none of which are of greater importance, than that the object on whom it is placed, should possess good sense—good dispositions—and the means of supporting you in the way you have been brought up. Such qualifications cannot fail to attract (after marriage) your esteem & regard, into wch or into disgust, sooner or later, love naturally resolves itself; and who at the sametime, has a claim to the respect, & esteem of the circle he moves in. Without these, whatever may be your first impressions of the man, they will end in disappointment; for be assured, and experience will convince you, that there is no truth more certain, than that all our enjoyments fall short of our expectations; and to none does it apply with more force, than to the gratification of the passions. You may believe me to be always, & sincerely Your Affectionate

Go: Washington

TO ALEXANDER HAMILTON (PRIVATE), JULY 29, 1795 (EXCERPT)
From Mount Vernon

In late July 1795, Washington was in the midst of a crisis. The Senate had conditionally ratified the Jay Treaty a month earlier, and it was not popular with the American people.

To avoid another war with Great Britain, Washington sent Supreme Court Chief Justice John Jay to London in 1794 to settle matters left over from the Revolutionary War and to set up negotiations concerning trade, shipping, commerce, land boundaries, and Britain's occupation of forts on America's frontier. (Great Britain, still at war with France, was restricting America's shipping and trade.) Many, especially the Democratic-Republicans, felt that the treaty favored Great Britain, left out certain important matters, and weakened the United States' relationship with France. Federalists, on the other hand, supported a strong relationship and peace with Great Britain. Hamilton, now a private citizen but still a staunch Federalist, was one of the treaty's most vocal supporters.

Although Washington had reservations about the treaty, by late July he accepted its provisions. In August, Washington returned to Philadelphia and signed the treaty. In late April 1796, the House voted the necessary funds to implement it.

> As the measures of the government, respecting the treaty, were taken before I left Philadelphia, something more imperious than has yet appeared, must turn up to occasion a change. Still, it is very desirable to ascertain, if possible, after the paroxysm of the fever is a little abated, what the real temper of the people is, concerning it; for at present the cry against the Treaty is like that against a mad-dog; and every one, in a manner, seems engaged in running it down.
>
> That it has received the most tortured interpretation, and that the writings agt. it (which are very industriously circulated) are pregnant of the most abominable mis-representations, admits of no doubt; yet, there are to be found, so far as my information extends, many well disposed men who conceive, that in the settlement of *old* disputes, a proper regard to reciprocal justice does not appear in the Treaty; whilst others, also well enough affected to the government, are of opinion that to have had *no* commercial treaty would have been better, for this country, than the restricted one, agreed to; inasmuch, say they, the nature of our Exports, and imports (without any extra: or violent measures) would have forced, or led to a more adequate intercourse between the two nations; without any of those shackles which the treaty has imposed. . . . But the string which is most played on, because it strikes with most force the popular ear, is the violation, as they term it, of our engagements with France; or in other words, the prediliction shown by that instrument to G. Britain at the expence of the French nation.

In 1796, Senator William Bingham of Pennsylvania and his wife, Anne, commissioned Gilbert Stuart to paint George Washington from life as a gift for British Lord Lansdowne, a friend of the patriot cause. The National Portrait Gallery in Washington, D.C., owns this painting. Other versions of the Lansdowne portrait exist either partly painted by Stuart or wholly by copyists. None of these were done from life. The Lansdowne portrait at right is at the Pennsylvania Academy of the Fine Arts and was painted for the Binghams. The Munro-Lenox portrait on the cover is similar to the Lansdowne portrait. It was done by Stuart but after Washington's death.

THE FAREWELL ADDRESS
UNITED STATES, SEPTEMBER 19, 1796

In 1796 Washington finally decided to retire. He had tried to retire after his first term, but many people in government convinced him that he was needed. Washington knew that he wanted to give the American people plenty of advance notice about his decision. His farewell address was first printed in *Claypoole's American Daily Advertiser*, a Philadelphia Federalist paper, in mid-September.

To write his farewell, Washington turned to the address he had written with James Madison's help in 1792. He also sought editorial help from Alexander Hamilton. Hamilton convinced him that the address should be less personal and concentrate more on the future needs of the country. Washington highlights the importance of independence and national unity over personal, party, sectional, and foreign interests.

Since 1893 the U.S. Senate has celebrated Washington's birthday every year with a reading of his political masterpiece.

Around 1814 William Rush carved this
life-size statue of George Washington out
of wood and then painted it off-white.

FRIENDS, & FELLOW-CITIZENS.

The period for a new election of a Citizen, to Administer the Executive government of the United States, being not far distant, and the time actually arrived, when your thoughts must be employed in designating the person, who is to be cloathed with that important trust, it appears to me proper, especially as it may conduce to a more distinct expression of the public voice, that I should now apprise you of the resolution I have formed, to decline being considered among the number of those, out of whom a choice is to be made.

I beg you, at the sametime, to do me the justice to be assured, that this resolution has not been taken, without a strict regard to all the considerations appertaining to the relation, which binds a dutiful Citizen to his country—and that, in withdrawing the tender of service which silence in my Situation might imply, I am influenced by no diminution of zeal for your future interest, no deficiency of grateful respect for your past kindness; but am supported by a full conviction that the step is compatible with both.

The acceptance of, & continuance hitherto in, the Office to which your Suffrages have twice called me, have been a uniform sacrifice of inclination to the opinion of duty, and to a deference for what appeared to be your desire. I constantly hoped, that it would have been much earlier in my power, consistently with motives, which I was not at liberty to disregard, to return to that retirement, from which I had been reluctantly drawn. The strength of my inclination to do this, previous to the last Election, had even led to the preparation of an address to declare it to you; but mature reflection on the then perplexed & critical posture of our Affairs with foreign nations, and the unanimous advice of persons entitled to my confidence, impelled me to abandon the idea.

I rejoice, that the state of your concerns, external as well as internal, no longer renders the pursuit of inclination incompatible with the sentiment of duty, or propriety; & am persuaded whatever partiality may be retained for my services, that in the present circumstances of our country, you will not disapprove my determination to retire.

The impressions, with which, I first undertook the arduous trust, were explained on the proper occasion. In the discharge of this trust, I will only say, that I have, with good intentions, contributed towards the Organization and Administration of the government, the best exertions of which a very fallible judgment was capable. Not unconscious, in the outset, of the inferiority of my qualifications, experience in my own eyes, perhaps still more in the eyes of others, has strengthned the motives to diffidence of myself; and every day the encreasing weight of years admonishes me more and more, that the shade of retirement is as necessary to me as it will be welcome. Satisfied that if any circumstances have given peculiar value to my services, they were temporary, I have the consolation to believe, that while choice and prudence invite me to quit the political scene, patriotizm does not forbid it.

In looking forward to the moment, which is intended to terminate the career of my public life, my feelings do not permit me to suspend the deep acknowledgment of that debt of gratitude wch I owe to my beloved country, for the many honors it has conferred upon me; still more for the stedfast confidence with which it has supported me; and for the opportunities I have thence enjoyed of manifesting my inviolable attachment, by services faithful & persevering, though in usefulness unequal to my zeal. If benefits have resulted to our country from these services, let it always be remembered to your praise, and as an instructive example in our annals, that, under circumstances in which the Passions agitated in every direction were liable to mislead, amidst appearances sometimes dubious, viscissitudes of fortune often discouraging, in situations in which not unfrequently want of Success has countenanced the spirit of criticism, the constancy of your support was the essential prop of the efforts, and a guarantee of the plans by which they were effected. Profoundly penetrated with this idea, I shall carry it with me to my grave, as a strong incitement to unceasing vows that Heaven may continue to you the choicest tokens of its beneficence—that your Union & brotherly affection may be perpetual—that the free constitution, which is the work of your hands, may be sacredly maintained—that its Administration in every department may be stamped with wisdom and Virtue—that, in fine, the happiness of the people of these States, under the auspices of liberty, may be made complete, by so careful a preservation and so prudent a use of this blessing as will acquire to them the glory of recommending it to the applause, the affection—and adoption of every nation which is yet a stranger to it.

Here, perhaps, I ought to stop. But a solicitude for your welfare, which cannot end but with my life, and the apprehension of danger, natural to that solicitude, urge me on an occasion like the present, to offer to your solemn contemplation, and to recommend to your frequent review, some sentiments; which are the result of much reflection, of no inconsiderable observation, and which appear to me all important to the permanency of your felicity as a People. These will be offered to you with the more freedom as you can only see in them the disinterested warnings of a parting friend, who can possibly have no personal motive to biass his counsel. Nor can I forget, as an encouragement to it, your endulgent reception of my sentiments on a former and not dissimilar occasion.

Interwoven as is the love of liberty with every ligament of your hearts, no recommendation of mine is necessary to fortify or confirm the Attachment.

The Unity of Government which constitutes you one people is also now dear to you. It is justly so; for it is a main Pillar in the Edifice of your real independence, the support of your tranquility at home; your peace abroad; of your safety; of your prosperity; of that very Liberty which you so highly prize. But as it is easy to foresee, that from different causes & from different quarters, much pains will be taken, many artifices employed, to weaken in your minds the conviction of this truth; as this is the point in your political fortress against which the batteries of internal & external enemies will be most constantly and actively (though often covertly & insidiously) directed, it is of infinite moment, that you should properly estimate the immense value of your national Union to your collective & individual happiness; that you should cherish a cordial, habitual & immoveable attachment to it; accustoming yourselves to think and speak of it as of the Palladium of your political safety and prosperity; watching for its preservation with jealous anxiety; discountenancing whatever may suggest even a suspicion that it can in any event be abandoned, and indignantly frowning upon the first dawning of every attempt to alienate any portion of our Country from the rest, or to enfeeble the sacred ties which now link together the various parts.

For this you have every inducement of sympathy and interest. Citizens by birth or choice, of a common country, that country has a right to concentrate your affections. The name of American, which belongs to you, in your national capacity, must always exalt the just pride of Patriotism, more than any appellation derived from local discriminations. With slight shades of difference, you have the same Religeon, Manners, Habits & political Principles. You have in a common cause fought & triumphed together—The independence & liberty you possess are the work of joint councils, and joint efforts—of common dangers, sufferings and successes.

But these considerations, however powerfully they address themselves to your sensibility are greatly outweighed by those which apply more immediately to your Interest. Here every portion of our country finds the most commanding motives for carefully guarding & preserving the Union of the whole.

The *North*, in an unrestrained intercourse with the *South*, protected by the equal Laws of a common government, finds in the productions of the latter, great additional resources of Maratime & commercial enterprise and—precious materials of manufacturing industry. The *South* in the same Intercourse, benefitting by the Agency of the *North*, sees its agriculture grow & its commerce expand. Turning partly into its own channels the seamen of the North, it finds its particular navigation envigorated; and while it contributes, in different ways, to nourish & increase the general mass of the National navigation, it looks forward to the protection of a Maratime strength, to which itself is unequally adapted. The *East*, in a like intercourse with the *West*, already finds, and in the progressive improvement of interior communications, by land & water, will more & more find a valuable vent for the commodities which it brings from abroad, or manufactures at home. The *West* derives from the *East* supplies requisite to its growth & comfort—and what is perhaps of still greater consequence, it must of necessity owe the Secure enjoyment of indispensable *outlets* for its own productions to the weight, influence, and the future maritime strength of the Atlantic side of the Union, directed by an indissoluble community of Interest as *one Nation*. Any other tenure by which the *West* can hold this essential advantage, whether derived from its own seperate strength, or from an apostate & unnatural connection with any foreign Power, must be intrinsically precarious.

While then every part of our country thus feels an immediate & particular Interest in Union, all the parts combined cannot fail to find in the united mass of means & efforts greater strength, greater resource, proportionably greater security from external danger, a less frequent interruption of their Peace by foreign Nations; and, what is of inestimable value! they must derive from Union an exemption from those broils and Wars between themselves, which so frequently afflict neighbouring countries, not tied together by the same government; which their own rivalships alone would be sufficient to produce, but which opposite foreign alliances, attachments & intriegues would stimulate & imbitter. Hence likewise they will avoid the necessity of those overgrown Military establishments, which under any form of Government are inauspicious to liberty, and which are to be regarded as particularly hostile to Republican Liberty: In this sense it is, that your union ought to be considered as a main prop of your liberty, and that the love of the one ought to endear to you the preservation of the other.

These considerations speak a persuasive language to every reflecting & virtuous mind, and exhibit the continuance of the Union as a primary object of Patriotic desire. Is there a doubt, whether a common government can embrace so large a sphere? Let experience solve it. To listen to mere speculation in such a case were criminal. We are authorized to hope that a proper organization of the whole, with the auxiliary agency of governments for the respective Subdivisions, will afford a happy issue to the experiment. 'Tis well worth a fair and full experiment. With such powerful and obvious motives to Union, affecting all parts of our country, while experience shall not have demonstrated its impracticability, there will always be reason, to distrust the patriotism of those, who in any quarter may endeavor to weaken its bands.

In contemplating the causes wch may disturb our Union, it occurs as matter of serious concern, that any ground should have been furnished for characterizing parties by *Geographical* discriminations—*Northern* and *Southern*—*Atlantic* and *Western;* whence designing men may endeavour to excite a belief that there is a real difference of local interests and views. One of the expedients of Party to acquire influence, within particular districts, is to misrepresent the opinions & aims of other Districts. You cannot shield yourselves too much against the jealousies & heart burnings which spring from these misrepresentations. They tend to render Alien to each other those who ought to be bound together by fraternal Affection. The Inhabitants of our Western country have lately had a useful lesson on this head. They have Seen, in the Negociation by the Executive, and in the unanimous ratification by the Senate, of the Treaty with Spain, and in the universal satisfaction at that event, throughout the United States, a decisive proof how unfounded were the suspicions propagated among them of a policy in the General Government and in the Atlantic States unfriendly to their Interests in regard to the Mississippi. They have been witnesses to the formation of two Treaties, that with G: Britain and that with Spain, which secure to them every thing they could desire, in respect to our Foreign relations, towards confirming their prosperity. Will it not be their wisdom to rely for the preservation of these advantages on the Union by wch they were procured? Will they not henceforth be deaf to those Advisers, if such there are, who would sever them from their Brethren and connect them with Aliens?

To the efficacy and permanency of Your Union, a Government for the whole is indispensable. No Alliances however strict between the parts can be an adequate substitute. They must inevitably experience the infractions & interruptions which all Alliances in all times have experienced. Sensible of this momentous truth, you have improved upon your first essay, by the adoption of a Constitution of Government, better calculated than your former for an intimate Union, and for the efficacious management of your common concerns. This government, the offspring of our own choice uninfluenced and unawed, adopted upon full investigation & mature deliberation, completely free in its principles, in the distribution of its powers, uniting security with energy, and containing within itself a provision for its own amendment, has a just claim to your confidence and your support. Respect for its authority, compliance with its Laws, acquiescence in its measures, are duties enjoined by the fundamental maxims of true Liberty. The basis of our political Systems is the right of the people to make and to alter their Constitutions of Government. But the Constitution which at any time exists, 'till changed by an explicit and authentic act of the whole People, is sacredly obligatory upon all. The very idea of the power and the right of the People to establish Government presupposes the duty of every Individual to obey the established Government.

All obstructions to the execution of the Laws, all combinations and Associations, under whatever plausible character, with the real design to direct, controul counteract, or awe the regular deliberation and action of the Constituted authorities are distructive of this fundamental principle and of fatal tendency. They serve to Organize faction, to give it an artificial and extraordinary force—to put in the place of the delegated will of the Nation, the will of a party; often a small but artful and enterprizing minority of the Community; and, according to the alternate triumphs of different parties, to make the public Administration the Mirror of the ill concerted and incongruous projects of faction, rather than the Organ of consistent and wholesome plans digested by common councils and modefied by mutual interests. However combinations or Associations of the above description may now & then answer popular ends, they are likely, in the course of time and things, to become potent engines, by which cunning, ambitious and unprincipled men will be enabled to subvert the Power of the People, & to usurp for themselves the reins of Government; destroying afterwards the very engines which have lifted them to unjust dominion.

Towards the preservation of your Government and the permanency of your present happy state, it is requisite, not only that you steadily discountenance irregular oppositions to its acknowledged authority, but also that you resist with care the spirit of innovation upon its principles however specious the pretexts. One method of assault may be to effect, in the forms of the Constitution, alterations which will impair the energy of the system, and thus to undermine what cannot be directly overthrown. In all the changes to which you may be invited, remember that time and habit are at least as necessary to fix the true character of Governments, as of other human institutions—that experience is the surest standard, by which to test the real tendency of the existing Constitution of a Country— that facility in changes upon the credit of mere hypotheses & opinion exposes to perpetual change, from the endless variety of hypotheses and opinion: and remember, especially, that for the efficient management of your common interests, in a country so extensive as ours, a Government of as much vigour as is consistent with the perfect security of Liberty is indispensable—Liberty itself will find in such a Government, with powers properly distributed and adjusted, its surest Guardian. It is indeed little else than a name, where the Government is too feeble to withstand the enterprises of faction, to confine each member of the Society within the limits prescribed by the laws & to maintain all in the secure & tranquil enjoyment of the rights of person & property.

I have already intimated to you the danger of Parties in the State, with particular reference to the founding of them on Geographical discriminations. Let me now take a more comprehensive view, & warn you in the most solemn manner against the baneful effects of the Spirit of Party, generally.

This Spirit, unfortunately, is inseperable from our nature, having its root in the strongest passions of the human Mind. It exists under different shapes in all Governments, more or less stifled, controuled, or repressed; but in those of the popular form it is seen in its greatest rankness and is truly their worst enemy.

The alternate domination of one faction over another, sharpened by the spirit of revenge natural to party dissention, which in different ages & countries has perpetrated the most horrid enormities, is itself a frightful despotism. But this leads at length to a more formal and permanent despotism. The disorders & miseries, which result, gradually incline the minds of men to seek security & repose in the absolute power of an Individual: and sooner or later the chief of some prevailing faction more able or more fortunate than his competitors, turns this disposition to the purposes of his own elevation, on the ruins of Public Liberty.

Without looking forward to an extremity of this kind (which nevertheless ought not to be entirely out of sight) the common & continual mischiefs of the spirit of Party are sufficient to make it the interest and the duty of a wise People to discourage and restrain it.

It serves always to distract the Public Councils and enfeeble the Public Administration. It agitates the Community with ill founded Jealousies and false alarms, kindles the animosity of one part against another, foments occasionally riot & insurrection. It opens the door to foreign influence & corruption, which find a facilitated access to the government itself through the channels of party passions. Thus the policy and the will of one country, are subjected to the policy and will of another.

There is an opinion that parties in free countries are useful checks upon the Administration of the Government and serve to keep alive the spirit of Liberty. This within certain limits is probably true—and in Governments of a Monarchical cast Patriotism may look with endulgence, if not with favour, upon the spirit of party. But in those of the popular character, in Governments purely elective, it is a spirit not to be encouraged. From their natural tendency, it is certain there will always be enough of that spirit for every salutary purpose. And there being constant danger of excess, the effort ought to be, by force of public opinion, to mitigate & assuage it. A fire not to be quenched; it demands a uniform vigilance to prevent its bursting into a flame, lest instead of warming it should consume.

It is important, likewise, that the habits of thinking in a free Country should inspire caution in those entrusted with its Administration, to confine themselves within their respective Constitutional Spheres; avoiding in the exercise of the Powers of one department to encroach upon another. The spirit of encroachment tends to consolidate the powers of all the departments in one, and thus to create whatever the form of government, a real despotism. A just estimate of that love of power, and proneness to abuse it, which predominates in the human heart, is sufficient to satisfy us of the truth of this position. The necessity of reciprocal checks in the exercise of political power; by dividing and distributing it into different depositories, & constituting each the Guardian of the Public Weal against invasions by the others, has been evinced by experiments ancient & modern; some of them in our country & under our own eyes. To preserve them must be as necessary as to institute them. If in the opinion of the People, the distribution or modification of the Constitutional powers be in any particular wrong, let it be corrected by an amendment in the way which the Constitution designates. But let there be no change by usurpation; for though this, in one instance, may be the instrument of good, it is the customary weapon by which free governments are destroyed. The precedent must always greatly overbalance in permanent evil any partial or transient benefit which the use can at any time yield.

Of all the dispositions and habits which lead to political prosperity, Religion and morality are indispensable supports. In vain would that man claim the tribute of Patriotism, who should labour to subvert these great Pillars of human happiness, these firmest props of the duties of Men & citizens. The mere Politican, equally with the pious man ought to respect & to cherish them. A volume could not trace all their connections with private & public felicity. Let it simply be asked where is the security for property, for reputation, for life, if the sense of religious obligation *desert* the Oaths, which are the instruments of investigation in Courts of Justice? And let us with caution indulge the supposition, that morality can be maintained without religion. Whatever may be conceded to the influence of refined education on minds of peculiar structure—reason & experience both forbid us to expect that National morality can prevail in exclusion of religious principle.

'Tis substantially true, that virtue or morality is a necessary spring of popular government. The rule indeed extends with more or less force to every species of Free Government. Who that is a sincere friend to it, can look with indifference upon attempts to shake the foundation of the fabric.

Promote then as an object of primary importance, Institutions for the general diffusion of knowledge. In proportion as the structure of a government gives force to public opinion, it is essential that public opinion should be enlightened.

As a very important source of strength & security, cherish public credit. One method of preserving it is to use it as sparingly as possible: avoiding occasions of expence by cultivating peace, but remembering also that timely disbursements to prepare for danger frequently prevent much greater disbursements to repel it—avoiding likewise the accumulation of debt, not only by shunning occasions of expence, but by vigorous exertions in time of Peace to discharge the Debts which unavoidable wars may have occasioned, not ungenerously throwing upon posterity the burthen which we ourselves ought to bear. The execution of these maxims belongs to your Representatives, but it is necessary that public opinion should cooperate. To facilitate to them the performance of their duty, it is essential that you should practically bear in mind, that towards the payment of debts there must be Revenue—that to have Revenue there must be taxes—that no taxes can be devised which are not more or less inconvenient & unpleasant—that the intrinsic embarrassment inseperable from the Selection of the proper objects (which is always a choice of difficulties) ought to be a decisive motive for a candid construction of the Conduct of the Government in making it, and for a spirit of acquiescence in the measures for obtaining Revenue which the public exigencies may at any time dictate.

Observe good faith & justice towds all Nations. Cultivate peace & harmony with all—Religion & morality enjoin this conduct; and can it be that good policy does not equally enjoin it? It will be worthy of a free, enlightened, and, at no distant period, a great Nation, to give to mankind the magnanimous and too novel example of a People always guided by an exalted justice & benevolence. Who can doubt that in the course of time and things the fruits of such a plan would richly repay any temporary advantages wch might be lost by a steady adherence to it? Can it be, that Providence has not connected the permanent felicity of a Nation with its virtue? The experiment, at least, is recommended by every sentiment which ennobles human Nature. Alas! is it rendered impossible by its vices?

In the execution of such a plan nothing is more essential than that permanent inveterate antipathies against particular Nations and passionate attachments for others should be excluded; and that in place of them just & amicable feelings towards all should be cultivated. The Nation, which indulges towards another an habitual hatred, or an habitual fondness, is in some degree a slave. It is a slave to its animosity or to its affection, either of which is sufficient to lead it astray from its duty and its interest.

Antipathy in one Nation against another—disposes each more readily to offer insult and injury, to lay hold of slight causes of umbrage, and to be haughty and intractable, when accidental or trifling occasions of dispute occur. Hence frequent collisions, obstinate envenomed and bloody contests. The Nation, prompted by ill will & resentment sometimes impels to War the Government, contrary to the best calculations of policy. The Government sometimes participates in the national propensity, and adopts through passion what reason would reject; at other times, it makes the animosity of the Nation subservient to projects of hostility instigated by pride, ambition and other sinister & pernicious motives. The peace often, sometimes perhaps the Liberty, of Nations has been the victim.

So likewise, a passionate attachment of one Nation for another produces a variety of evils. Sympathy for the favourite nation, facilitating the illusion of an imaginary common interest, in cases where no real common interest exists, and infusing into one the enmities of the other, betrays the former into a participation in the quarrels & Wars of the latter, without adequate inducement or justification: It leads also to concessions to the favourite Nation of priviledges denied to others, which is apt doubly to injure the Nation making the concessions—by unnecessarily parting with what ought to have been retained—& by exciting jealousy, ill will, and a disposition to retaliate, in the parties from whom eql priviledges are withheld: And it gives to ambitious, corrupted, or deluded citizens (who devote themselves to the favourite Nation) facility to betray, or sacrifice the interests of their own country, without odium, sometimes even with popularity; gilding with the appearances of a virtuous sense of obligation a commendable deference for public opinion, or a laudable zeal for public good, the base or foolish compliances of ambition corruption or infatuation.

As avenues to foreign influence in innumerable ways, such attachments are particularly alarming to the truly enlightened and independent Patriot. How many opportunities do they afford to tamper with domestic factions, to practice the arts of seduction, to mislead public opinion, to influence or awe the public Councils! Such an attachment of a small or weak, towards a great & powerful Nation, dooms the former to be the satellite of the latter.

Against the insidious wiles of foreign influence, (I conjure you to believe me fellow citizens,), the jealousy of a free people ought to be *constantly* awake; since history and experience prove that foreign influence is one of the most baneful foes of Republican Government. But that jealousy to be useful must be impartial; else it becomes the instrument of the very influence to be avoided, instead of a defence against it. Excessive partiality for one foreign nation and excessive dislike of another, cause those whom they actuate to see danger only on one side, and serve to veil and even second the arts of influence on the other. Real Patriots, who may resist the intriegues of the favourite, are liable to become suspected and odious; while its tools and dupes usurp the applause & confidence of the people, to surrender their interests.

The Great rule of conduct for us, in regard to foreign Nations is in extending our comercial relations to have with them as little *political* connection as possible. So far as we have already formed engagements let them be fulfilled, with perfect good faith. Here let us stop.

Europe has a set of primary interests, which to us have none, or a very remote relation. Hence she must be engaged in frequent controversies, the causes of which are essentially foreign to our concerns. Hence therefore it must be unwise in us to implicate ourselves, by artificial ties, in the ordinary vicissitudes of her politics, or the ordinary combinations & collisions of her friendships, or enmities.

Our detached & distant situation invites and enables us to pursue a different course. If we remain one People, under an efficient government, the period is not far off, when we may defy material injury from external annoyance; when we may take such an attitude as will cause the neutrality we may at any time resolve upon to be scrupulously respected; when belligerent nations, under the impossibility of making acquisitions upon us, will not lightly hazard the giving us provocation; when we may choose peace or War, as our interest guided by justice shall Counsel.

Why forego the advantages of so peculiar a situation? Why quit our own to stand upon foreign ground? Why, by interweaving our destiny with that of any part of Europe, entangle our peace and prosperity in the toils of European Ambition, Rivalship, Interest, Humour or Caprice?

'Tis our true policy to steer clear of permanent Alliances, with any portion of the foreign World—So far, I mean, as we are now at liberty to do it—for let me not be understood as capable of patronising infidility to existing engagements, (I hold the maxim no less applicable to public than to private affairs, that honesty is always the best policy)—I repeat it therefore, Let those engagements. be observed in their genuine sense. But in my opinion, it is unnecessary and would be unwise to extend them.

Taking care always to keep ourselves, by suitable establishments, on a respectably defensive posture, we may safely trust to temporary alliances for extraordinary emergencies.

Harmony, liberal intercourse with all Nations, are recommended by policy, humanity and interest. But even our Commercial policy should hold an equal and impartial hand: neither seeking nor granting exclusive favours or preferences; consulting the natural course of things; diffusing & deversifying by gentle means the streams of Commerce, but forcing nothing; establishing with Powers so disposed—in order to give to trade a stable course, to define the rights of our Merchants, and to enable the Government to support them—conventional rules of intercourse; the best that present circumstances and mutual opinion will permit, but temporary, & liable to be from time to time abandoned or varied, as experience and circumstances shall dictate; constantly keeping in view, that 'tis folly in one Nation to look for disinterested favors from another—that it must pay with a portion of its Independence for whatever it may accept under that character—that by such acceptance, it may place itself in the condition of having given equivalents for nominal favours and yet of being reproached with ingratitude for not giving more. There can be no greater error than to expect, or calculate upon real favours from Nation to Nation. 'Tis an illusion which experience must cure, which a just pride ought to discard.

In offering to you, my Countrymen, these counsels of an old and affectionate friend, I dare not hope they will make the strong and lasting impression, I could wish—that they will controul the usual current of the passions, or prevent our Nation from running the course which has hitherto marked the Destiny of Nations: But if I may even flatter myself, that they may be productive of some partial benefit, some occasional good; that they may now & then recur to moderate the fury of party spirit, to warn against the mischiefs of foreign Intriegue, to guard against the Impostures of pretended patriotism—this hope will be a full recompence for the solicitude for your welfare, by which they have been dictated.

How far in the discharge of my Official duties, I have been guided by the principles which have been delineated, the public Records and other evidences of my conduct must witness to You and to the world. To myself, the assurance of my own conscience is, that I have at least believed myself to be guided by them.

In relation to the still subsisting War in Europe, my Proclamation of the 22d of April 1793 is the index to my Plan. Sanctioned by your approving voice and by that of Your Representatives in both Houses of Congress, the spirit of that measure has continually governed me; uninfluenced by any attempts to deter or divert me from it.

After deliberate examination with the aid of the best lights I could obtain I was well satisfied that our Country, under all the circumstances of the case, had a right to take, and was bound in duty and interest, to take a Neutral position. Having taken it, I determined, as far as should depend upon me, to maintain it, with moderation, perseverence & firmness.

The considerations, which respect the right to hold this conduct, it is not necessary on this occasion to detail. I will only observe, that according to my understanding of the matter, that right, so far from being denied by any of the Belligerent Powers has been virtually admitted by all.

The duty of holding a neutral conduct may be inferred, without any thing more, from the obligation which justice and humanity impose on every Nation, in cases in which it is free to act, to maintain inviolate the relations of Peace and amity towards other Nations.

The inducements of interest for observing that conduct will best be referred to your own reflections & experience. With me, a predominant motive has been to endeavour to gain time to our country to settle & mature its yet recent institutions, and to progress without interruption, to that degree of strength & consistency, which is necessary to give it, humanly speaking, the command of its own fortunes.

Though in reviewing the incidents of my Administration, I am unconscious of intentional error—I am nevertheless too sensible of my defects not to think it probable that I may have committed many errors. Whatever they may be I fervently beseech the Almighty to avert or mitigate the evils to which they may tend. I shall also carry with me the hope that my Country will never cease to view them with indulgence; and that after forty five years of my life dedicated to its Service, with an upright zeal, the faults of incompetent abilities will be consigned to oblivion, as myself must soon be to the Mansions of rest.

Relying on its kindness in this as in other things, and actuated by that fervent love towards it, which is so natural to a Man, who views in it the native soil of himself and his progenitors for several Generations; I anticipate with pleasing expectation that retreat, in which I promise myself to realize, without alloy, the sweet enjoyment of partaking, in the midst of my fellow Citizens, the benign influence of good Laws under a free Government—the ever favourite object of my heart, and the happy reward, as I trust, of our mutual cares, labours and dangers.

Go: Washington

CHAPTER SEVEN

THE RETIRED PRESIDENT

A View of Mount Vernon was published in England in 1798, a year before Washington's death.

TO JAMES MCHENRY,* APRIL 3, 1797 (EXCERPT)
TO TOBIAS LEAR,** JULY 31, 1797

From Mount Vernon

At THE END OF HIS SECOND PRESIDENTIAL TERM in March 1797, Washington returned to Mount Vernon and found much to do and many people to entertain—family, friends, and people interested in simply meeting the great man.

Life at Mount Vernon was anything but relaxing, but when Washington

---

*Secretary of War
**Lear had served Washington as secretary and tutor from 1786–1793. He returned to work for Washington in 1798 and was with him when he died.*

made daily rounds to check up on his many fields, workers, and farms, he found peace and quiet.

Washington writes about building a place to house his papers—something like a presidential library—but it was never built.

> I find myself in the situation, nearly, of a young beginner, for although I have not houses to build (except one, which I must erect for the accomodation & security of my Military, Civil & private Papers, which are voluminous and may be interesting) yet I have not one, or scarcely any thing else about me that does not require considerable repairs. In a word, I am already surrounded by Joiners, Masons, Painters &ca &ca and such is my anxiety to get out of their hands, that I have scarcely a room to put a friend into, or to set in myself, without the Music of hammers, or the odoriferous smell of Paint.

<hr />

Dear Sir

I am alone *at present,* and shall be glad to see you this evening.

Unless some one pops in, unexpectedly, Mrs Washington and myself will do what I believe has not been [done] within the last twenty years by us, that is to set down to dinner by ourselves. I am Yr afffectionate

Go: Washington

James Sharples, an English artist, created pastel portraits of Washington that members of the artist's family copied. This pastel on paper, probably by Sharples's wife, Ellen, is at the Independence National Historical Park.

TO JAMES MCHENRY, JULY 4, 1798 (EXCERPT)
From Mount Vernon

Although retired from public office, Washington still knew what was going on in the country, thanks to a correspondence with Secretary of War James McHenry and others and through discussions with the many guests at Mount Vernon. In the summer of 1798, France was threatening war with the United States. The French resented the Jay Treaty (see pages 91–92), had made several attacks on American shipping, and were disillusioned with the breakdown of communication with the United States.

Washington had an idea that he might be called back into service as commander in chief. And as so many times in the past, he was willing to sacrifice his personal life and retirement to serve his country. This time, however, Washington set certain conditions. He wanted to make sure that the public did not mind his age and his coming out of retirement, that it supported his appointment, and that if he took on the command he would be surrounded by competent officers and staff. More than ever, Washington was worried about reputation and honor.

He didn't know yet that he had already been commissioned as lieutenant general and commander in chief of the American forces. When he accepted the position in mid-July, Washington insisted that he remain out of the field of action until a French invasion seemed likely. Fortunately, that didn't happen, and a land war with France never came.

> The sentiments which I mean to express to you in this letter, on the subject of yours, shall be frank, undisguised & explicit; for I see, as you do, that Clouds are gathering, and that a Storm may ensue. And I find too, from a variety of hints, that my quiet under these circumstances, does not promise to be of long continuance.
>
> It cannot be necessary for me to premise to you, or to others who know my sentiments as well, that to quit the tranquil walks of retirement, and enter the boundless field of responsibility and trouble, would be productive of Sensations which a better pen than I possess would find it difficult to describe. Nevertheless, the principle by which my conduct has been actuated through life, would not suffer me, in any great emer-

gency, to withhold any services I could render, required by my Country; especially in a case where its dearest rights are assailed by lawless ambition and intoxicated power; contrary to every principle of justice, & in violation of solemn compact, & Laws which govern all Civilized Nations. And this too with obvious intent to sow thick the Seeds of disunion for the purpose of subjugating the Government, and destroying our Independence & happiness.

Under circumstance like these, accompanied by an actual Invasion of our territorial rights, it would be difficult for me, at any time, to remain an idle spectator under the plea of Age or Retirement. With sorrow, it is true, I should quit the shades of my peaceful abode; and the ease & happiness I now enjoy, to encounter anew the turmoils of War; to which, possibly, my strength and powers might be found incompetent. These, however, should not be stumbling blocks in my *own* way; but there are other things highly important for me to ascertain, & settle, before I could give a decided answer to your question.

First. The propriety, in the opinion of the public (so far as that opinion has been expressed in conversation) of my appearing again on a Public theatre, after delivering the sentiments I did, in my Valedictory Address of September 1796 [see pages 93–110].

Second. A conviction in my own breast (from the best information that can be obtained) that it is the wish of my Country that the Military force of it should be committed to my charge—and

Third. That the Army *now to be formed* should be so appointed as to afford a well grounded hope of its doing honor to the Country, & credit to him who Commands it, in the field.

The next year at least one of Washington's correspondents suggested that he seek a third presidential term. Washington, however, was not interested. For the few remaining years of his life he lived at his beloved Mount Vernon.

Washington and Martha Dandridge Custis Washington were married for more than forty years.

GEORGE WASHINGTON'S LAST WILL AND TESTAMENT, JULY 9, 1799 (EXCERPT)

In the summer of 1799, Washington decided to write a new will—alone with no legal help. The will took up twenty-nine pages. Historians are not sure about Washington's earlier wills, but they do know that he drafted a will shortly before he headed to Cambridge in 1775. Washington's last will is beautifully written and is considered to be one of his most important documents.

The bulk of Washington's estate went to Martha. Upon her death, the estate was to be divided among family. Most of the Mount Vernon plantation, along with his papers and library, went to his nephew Bushrod Washington. Gold-headed canes, furniture, spyglasses, and a Bible were given to friends. Lafayette received two "finely wrought steel Pistols" and Tobias Lear the use of one of his farms. Washington also left money for a free school and an academy and the establishment of a national university. Unfortunately, a national university was never built, but the academy later became Washington and Lee University.

The will's most memorable passage deals with Washington's plans for his slaves. Washington was the only Founding Father to free his slaves. After his death, the will was printed and distributed throughout the country. Washington's thoughts on slavery were no longer private.

Upon the decease <of> my wife, it is my Will & desire th<at> all the Slaves which I hold in <my> *own right*, shall receive their free<dom>. To emancipate them during <her> life, would, tho' earnestly wish<ed by> me, be attended with such insu<pera>ble difficulties on account of thei<r interm>ixture by Marriages with the <dow>er Negroes,* as to excite the most pa<in>ful sensations, if not disagreeabl<e c>onsequences from the latter, while <both> descriptions are in the occupancy <of> the same Proprietor; it not being <in> my power, under the tenure by which <th>e Dower Negroes are held, to man<umi>t them. And whereas among <thos>e who will recieve freedom ac<cor>ding to this devise, there may b<e so>me, who from old age or bodily infi<rm>ities, and others who on account of <the>ir infancy, that will be unable to <su>pport themselves; it is m<y Will and de>sire that all who <come under the first> & second descrip<tion shall be comfor>tably cloathed & <fed by my heirs while> they live; and that such of the latter description as have no parents living, or if living are unable, or unwilling to provide for them, shall be bound by the Court until they shall arrive at the ag<e> of twenty five years; and in cases where no record can be produced, whereby their ages can be ascertained, the judgment of the Court, upon its own view of the subject, shall be adequate and final. The Negroes thus bound, are (by their Masters or Mistresses) to be taught to read & write; and to be brought up to some useful occupation, agreeably to the Laws of the Commonwealth of Virginia, providing for the support of Orphan and other poor Children. and I do hereby expressly forbid the Sale, or transportation out of the said Commonwealth, of any Slave I may die possessed of, under any pretence whatsoever. And I do moreover most pointedly, and most solemnly enjoin it upon my Executors hereafter named, or the Survivors of them, to see that th<is cla>use respecting Slaves, and every part thereof be religiously fulfilled at the Epoch at which it is directed to take place; without evasion, neglect or delay, after

---

*These slaves were owned by Martha Washington as part of her inheritance from her first husband.

the Crops which may then be on the ground are harvested, particularly as it respects the aged and infirm; seeing that a regular and permanent fund be established for their support so long as there are subjects requiring it; not trusting to the <u>ncertain provision to be made by individuals. And to my Mulatto man William (calling himself William Lee) I give immediate freedom; or if he should prefer it (on account of the accidents which ha<v>e befallen him, and which have rendered him incapable of walking or of any active employment) to remain in the situation he now is, it shall be optional in him to do so: In either case however, I allow him an annuity of thirty dollars during his natural life, whic<h> shall be independent of the victuals and cloaths he has been accustomed to receive, if he chuses the last alternative; but in full, with his freedom, if he prefers the first; & this I give him as a test<im>ony of my sense of his attachment to me, and for his faithful services during the Revolutionary War.

Washington died at Mount Vernon on December 14, 1799. This illustration is by Felix Octavius Carr (F.O.C.) Darley, who lived from 1821 to 1888. Another illustration by Darley is on page 54.

DIARY ENTRIES, DECEMBER 12 AND 13, 1799

On the twelfth of December 1799, Washington went on his daily rounds to inspect his farms despite freezing cold, wind, and snow. The next day he complained of a sore throat and opted not to make his routine rounds. Washington went outside only briefly to mark some trees that needed to be cut. Always the farmer and planter, Washington faithfully recorded the weather conditions in his diary. He wrote his last letter on the thirteenth to James Anderson, his farm manager.

12. Morning Cloudy—Wind at No. Et. & Mer. 33. A large circle round the Moon last Night. About 1 oclock it began to snow—soon after to Hail and then turned to a settled cold Rain. Mer. 28 at Night.

13. Morning Snowing & abt. 3 Inches deep. Wind at No. Et. & Mer. at 30. Contg. Snowing till 1 Oclock and abt. 4 it became perfectly clear. Wind in the same place but not hard. Mer. 28 at Night.

In the early hours of the fourteenth, Washington complained of a violent sore throat and fever. That day he became much worse. He remained in bed, getting up only twice to sit by a fire. Despite the attentions of an overseer, three doctors, servants, Martha, and Tobias Lear, Washington knew death was near. "Docter, I die hard, but I am not afraid to go, I believed from my first attack that I shd not survive it, my breath cannot last long." Washington made sure his affairs were in order and that his burial would take place in not less than two days after his death. (Washington was worried about being buried alive.) He asked Martha to burn an old will and safeguard the new one.

Washington faced death as he did life—bravely and well prepared. After whispering "Tis well," Washington took his own pulse and died. Tobias Lear wrote two accounts of Washington's death. For him, Washington's "patience, fortitude & resignation never foresook him for a moment. In all his distress he uttered not a sigh nor a complaint, always endeavoring to take what was offered him, or to do what was desired."

Washington was buried in the family vault at Mount Vernon four days after his death.

IMPORTANT DATES

Residence of the Washington Family

1732—George Washington is born on February 22, the first child of Augustine Washington and his second wife, Mary Ball Washington. Washington has two half brothers—Lawrence, born in 1718, and Augustine, born in 1720—and one half sister, Jane, born in 1722. The Washington family lives in a small house near Pope's Creek along the Potomac River in Westmoreland County, Virginia. The house would later be known as Wakefield Farm.

1735—Jane dies. The family moves to a farmhouse, Epsewasson, at Little Hunting Creek on the Potomac River in Virginia. Lawrence Washington would live there as an adult and call his house Mount Vernon after British Admiral Edward Vernon, under whom he served during the Cartagena campaign.

1738—The family moves to Ferry Farm on the Rappahannock River across from Fredericksburg, Virginia.

1739—Sister Mildred is born. She will die the next year.

Lawrence Washington, 1718–1752

1743—Augustine Washington dies, leaving Mary to raise their five children—George, Betty (born in 1733), Samuel (born in 1734), John Augustine (born in 1736), and Charles (born in 1738). Washington inherits Ferry Farm, some land, ten slaves, and three town lots.

1748—In March, Washington leaves on a surveying trip to inspect lands for Lord Fairfax in Virginia's Northern Neck. Later in the year, Sarah "Sally" Fairfax weds George William Fairfax and moves to Belvoir, the estate next to Mount Vernon. The Fairfaxes and Washingtons remain great friends throughout Washington's lifetime.*

1750—Washington buys land on Bullskin Creek, a tributary of the Shenandoah in Frederick County, Virginia. Two years later, he will own more than a thousand acres of land there.

1751—Washington accompanies Lawrence to Barbados to seek a cure for Lawrence's tuberculosis. Washington contracts smallpox but recovers. He attends the theater for the first time. This is Washington's only trip out of the country. He keeps a diary of the voyage and his time spent on the island.

1752—Lawrence dies in July. In November, Washington joins the Masonic Lodge in Fredericksburg. (He becomes a Master Mason in 1753 and remains one for the rest of his life.) The next month Washington serves as adjutant with the rank of major in one of Virginia's military districts.

1753—Washington volunteers to deliver a message from Virginia's lieutenant governor, Robert Dinwiddie, to the French at Fort Le Boeuf.*

1754—As a lieutenant colonel, Washington heads back to the frontier, where he is involved in a skirmish with the French that begins the French and Indian War. Washington and his men build Fort Necessity at Great Meadows, Pennsylvania. In July, Washington surrenders to the French after a battle at the fort. Washington resigns from the Virginia regiment. He leases Mount Vernon from Lawrence's widow, Anne Fairfax, agreeing to pay her in tobacco—15,000 pounds a year—or the equivalent amount in cash for rent.*

1754—In the spring, the French build Fort Duquesne on a site where the Allegheny and Monongahela Rivers meet (the Forks of the Ohio River). They will burn and abandon the fort in 1758, allowing the British to erect Fort Pitt on or close to the site. (William Pitt was the prime minister of England at this time.)

---

*Indicates that there is a related paper or papers.

1755—Washington volunteers to serve as an aide to British General Edward Braddock. The Braddock campaign fails in its attack on the French. Washington, however, is considered a hero. In late summer he is put in charge of Virginia's forces.*

1758—After suffering defeats in 1755 and 1757, Washington is finally elected to Virginia's House of Burgesses. (He will be elected again in 1761, 1765, 1768, 1769, 1771, and 1774.) In December, Washington resigns his commission as commander of Virginia's forces.*

1759—On January 6, Washington marries Martha Dandridge Custis, a rich widow with two children, 300 slaves, and 18,000 acres of land. Washington completes one story and two additions to the sides of Mount Vernon. (He began the project in 1757.) He will start to make more changes and improvements to Mount Vernon and the surrounding grounds in 1775, completing them in 1786.*

1759–1760—Washington purchases more land around Mount Vernon. Eventually, he will own more than 8,000 acres and operate four working farms. Mansion House Farm, where the family lives, is not a working farm.

George III was the British king during the Revolutionary War.

1760—George III becomes king of Great Britain and Ireland and reigns for more than fifty years.

1761—Anne Fairfax dies, allowing Washington to own Mount Vernon.

1762—Washington becomes a vestryman of Truro Parish in Fairfax County, Virginia. (Vestrymen are elected to run the nonreligious affairs of the church.) In the 1760s, Washington mostly attends Pohick Church, one of the churches in the parish, seven miles from Mount Vernon. Washington also serves as a warden, or officer, of the church. He is actively involved with the construction plans of a new Pohick Church, which will begin in the late 1760s. After the war, Washington most often attends Christ Church in Alexandria, where he is also a vestryman.

1763—The Seven Years' War in Europe, of which the French and Indian War in North America was a small part, ends with the signing of the Treaty of Paris. The British victory allows them to take over almost all of France's possessions in North America.

1765—The British need to raise money to pay for the French and Indian War. The Stamp Act goes into effect. It will be repealed the next year.

1767—The British impose the Townshend Acts on the colonies. Duties are placed on certain imported goods, and an agency is set up to make sure the duties are paid. The colonists protest and boycott imported British goods. At Mount Vernon, Washington depends less on growing tobacco and more on wheat and corn.*

Boston Massacre, 1770

1768—Boston is a hotbed of colonial protest. British troops are sent there to maintain order.

1770—In March, British soldiers kill five colonists in Boston (the Boston Massacre). The next month, the Townshend duties are repealed, except for a tax on tea. Washington explores western lands owed him for fighting in the French and Indian War.

1773—The British Parliament enforces the Tea Act, which enables the British East India Company to undersell tea brought into America from other countries. The colonists protest. On June 19, Washington's stepdaughter, Patsy, dies. Late in the year, in Massachusetts, colonists dump British tea into Boston's harbor (the Boston Tea Party).*

Boston Tea Party, 1773

1774—The British enforce the Coercive Acts (known as the

Carpenters' Hall, Philadelphia

Intolerable Acts in the colonies). Boston's port is closed. Lieutenant General Thomas Gage, commander of the British forces in North America, becomes royal governor of Massachusetts. In July, Washington attends a meeting in Fairfax County, Virginia, that adopts the Fairfax Resolves. The Resolves were written by George Mason and Washington in response to what was happening in Massachusetts. They promote a boycott of British goods and the right to self-government for the colonies. From September to October, the First Continental Congress meets in Carpenters' Hall in Philadelphia. Washington is one of the seven delegates from Virginia.

1775—The Revolutionary War begins in Massachusetts. In April, battles take place in the towns of Lexington and Concord and in June at Breed's Hill in Charlestown, near Boston. In May, Ethan Allen, Benedict Arnold, and the Green Mountain Boys seize Fort Ticonderoga while Seth Warner and other Green Mountain Boys take Crown Point. (Both New York forts hold British artillery.) From May to June, Washington attends the Second Continental Congress (often in uniform) and is elected to command the Continental forces. In June, General Washington travels to Cambridge, across the Charles River from Boston, to assume command of the troops. In August, King George III declares the colonies to be in a state of rebellion.*

Unfortunately, when Washington took command of the troops in Cambridge, Massachusetts in 1775, things were not as orderly as this artist makes them out to be.

1775–1776—In November 1775, Continental troops occupy Montreal but are unable to take Quebec in late 1775 to early 1776.

1776—In January, *Common Sense*, a pamphlet by Thomas Paine promoting independence, is published. By April, Washington and his troops are in New York. The Continental Congress adopts the Declaration of

Independence on July 4. Five days later, Washington has it read to his troops. For the colonists, the war is now a fight for independence. In August, the Continental army suffers defeat at the Battle of Long Island. On December 25 and 26, Washington and his troops cross the Delaware River and attack Hessian soldiers at Trenton, New Jersey. Washington takes Trenton, his first major victory.*

General Horatio Gates

1777—Washington's second major victory takes place in January at the Battle of Princeton in New Jersey. He and his troops then move to Morristown, New Jersey, where they will remain until May. In the summer, Lafayette joins the Continental army as a major general. In late summer and early fall, Washington suffers defeats at the Battles of Brandywine and Germantown in Pennsylvania. The commander of the Northern Department, General Horatio Gates, on the other hand, is victorious at the Battle of Saratoga in New York, forcing the surrender of British General Burgoyne. (The Patriot victory at Saratoga helps convince France to enter into an alliance with the United States in February 1778.) In November, the Articles of Confederation are adopted. (It will take until 1781 before they are ratified by the states and put into effect.) In late December, Washington and his troops begin their six-month stay at Valley Forge, Pennsylvania.*

Washington's camp chest

1778—In May, the Continental Congress ratifies the Treaty of Alliance with France. France publicly joins the Patriot cause by supplying manpower and ships. (For two years France has secretly given the colonies arms, ammunition, and supplies.) Spain and the Netherlands also will supply substantial aid to the American cause over the next two years. In June, Washington and his troops meet the British near Freehold, New Jersey. (The Battle of Monmouth's outcome is indecisive as no defeat is acknowledged by the British.) That winter, Washington sets up his headquarters at the Wallace House in present-day Somerville, New Jersey. The Continental army is stationed at the Middlebrook encampment. In late December, the British capture Savannah, Georgia.

1779—George Rogers Clark and his troops defeat the British at Vincennes, Indiana.

1779–1780—Washington and his men spend the harshest winter of the war and of the century at Morristown, New Jersey.

1780—In May, the British capture Charleston, South Carolina, and in August, they defeat Horatio Gates, commander of the Southern Department, at Camden, South Carolina.

On October 19, 1781, Cornwallis formally surrendered to General Washington.

1781—In the South, the Continental forces defeat the British at the Cowpens in South Carolina. Although other Continental troops are defeated at the Battle of Guilford Courthouse in North Carolina, the British suffer many casualties. Later in the year, Washington, with help from the French, defeats British General Charles, Lord Cornwallis at Yorktown. Cornwallis formally surrenders on October 19. About two weeks later, Washington's stepson, John Parke Custis, dies.*

1783—In March, at Newburgh, New York, Washington addresses the complaints—mostly about back pay and pensions—of his officers, who are threatening to mutiny. Washington delivers a moving, theatrical speech and wins their sympathies. They do not mutiny. The Treaty of Paris is signed on September 3. From late August until early November, Washington writes his farewell orders to his troops in Rocky Hill, New Jersey, and attends congressional meetings held nearby in Princeton. In late November, Washington enters New York City after the British have been evacuated, and on December 4 he says good-bye to his officers at Fraunces Tavern. He then travels to Annapolis, Maryland, to resign his commission. By Christmas Eve, Washington is with Martha at Mount Vernon.*

Washington said good-bye to his officers at Fraunces Tavern in New York City on December 4, 1783.

1785—Washington becomes president of the Potomac Navigation Company. The company is interested in linking the Potomac River to the Ohio River so that supplies and goods can be transported between the East and the new western territories.

1786—In August, Daniel Shays and a group of farmers in western Massachusetts lead a revolt against high taxes and their state's financial policies. (State troops are eventually called in to stop the rebels.) Washington strongly opposes Shays's Rebellion. In September, the Annapolis Convention takes place to discuss commercial issues between the states and the need to organize a national convention to address changes to the Articles of Confederation.*

1787—From May until September, the Constitutional Convention is held in Philadelphia, with Washington presiding as president. The Constitution is signed in September, forwarded to Congress, and then sent to the states for ratification. Many essays are written for and against the ratification of the Constitution. Beginning in October, essays that support the Constitution and ratification are first published in New York newspapers. These eighty-five essays are known as the *Federalist Papers* (1787–1788).*

1788—On June 21, New Hampshire becomes the ninth state to ratify the Constitution. Four days later, Virginia ratifies it.*

John Adams served as the first vice president of the United States

1789—In February, Washington is unanimously elected the country's first president. John Adams is vice president. On March 4, the Constitution officially goes into effect. In the middle of April, Washington leaves Mount Vernon without Martha. He travels through a number of cities and towns to New York City, where on April 30 he takes the oath of office. Washington moves into a house on Cherry Street. Martha joins him in May. That summer, Mary Ball Washington dies in Fredericksburg, Virginia. In the fall, Washington tours Connecticut, Massachusetts, and New Hampshire. (He will tour Rhode Island the next year.) The Bill of Rights is adopted and sent to the states for ratification.*

1789—A revolution erupts in France, creating political turmoil and radical change. The king is suspended in 1792 and executed in January 1793. The revolution will rage for ten years.

1790—Washington delivers the first of eight annual addresses to the House of Representatives and the Senate. In the fall, the capital of the United States is relocated to Philadelphia; Washington moves into the house of Robert Morris.*

1791—In January, Washington selects an area on the Potomac River as the location for the nation's capital. It will be called Washington. During the spring, Washington tours the South, passing through Delaware, Virginia, North Carolina, South Carolina, and Georgia. (This trip and the earlier trips to New England and Rhode Island are taken to promote national unity.) At the end of the year, the Bill of Rights is ratified.

1792—Washington is unanimously reelected for a second term. Adams is again his vice president.

1793—France is at war with Britain and other European powers. Except for a brief period, they will remain at war until 1815. Washington issues his Proclamation of Neutrality.*

1794—Western Pennsylvanians revolt against an unfair tax on whiskey. President Washington organizes an army of 12,000 men, who put an end to the "Whiskey Rebellion." (The insurgents' trials drag on through much of 1795, and most of the accused are acquitted for lack of evidence. On July 10, 1795, Washington issues a proclamation that pardons most of those who were not acquitted or under indictment. Washington eventually pardons Philip Vigol and John Mitchell, the only men convicted of treason.) On November 19, Great Britain and the United States sign the Jay Treaty in England.*

1795—On October 27, Spain and the United States sign Pinckney's Treaty, or the Treaty of San Lorenzo, in Spain. The treaty allows the United States to navigate the Mississippi River and to deposit goods and conduct business in New Orleans, Louisiana. (Washington refers to this treaty as "the Treaty with Spain" in his Farewell Address—see pages 93–110.)

1796—In September, Washington's Farewell Address is printed in a Philadelphia newspaper.*

1797—In March, John Adams is sworn in as the country's second president. Thomas Jefferson is vice president. Washington and Martha return to Mount Vernon to live as private citizens. They will never live anywhere else.*

1798—The United States fears war with France. Washington is commissioned as lieutenant general and commander in chief of the army, but a land war with France never comes.*

1799—Washington dies at Mount Vernon with Martha at his bedside.*

In 1800, Washington, D.C., became the nation's capital. This view is looking down Pennsylvania Avenue.

1800—President John Adams and Abigail Adams move into the White House, which is still under construction. Washington, D.C., officially becomes the U.S. capital.

1802—Martha dies at Mount Vernon and is buried in the family vault with her husband.

1811—Sally Fairfax dies at the age of eighty-one in England.

1812—Less than thirty years after the signing of the Treaty of Paris, the United States is again at war with England. The War of 1812 ends in 1815, when the U.S. Senate ratifies the Treaty of Ghent.

1848—Construction begins on the Washington Monument in Washington, D.C. It will take forty years before the monument is open to the public.

1858—The Mount Vernon Ladies' Association buys Mount Vernon and 200 acres for $200,000. The mission of the association is to restore and maintain the house as well as surrounding buildings and grounds and to educate the public.

BIBLIOGRAPHY/ FURTHER RESOURCES

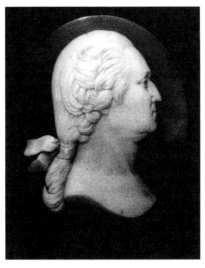

Around 1875, Augustus Saint-Gaudens (1848-1907) carved this portrait of Washington out of shell.

CHILDREN AND YOUNG ADULT BOOKS

Bruns, Roger. *World Leaders Past and Present: George Washington*. New York: Chelsea House Publishers, 1987.

Freedman, Russell. *Give Me Liberty! The Story of the Declaration of Independence*. New York: Holiday House, 2000.

Fritz, Jean. *George Washington's Breakfast*. New York: The Putnam & Grosset Group, 1969.

———. *George Washington's Mother*. New York: Grosset & Dunlap, 1992.

Giblin, James Cross. *George Washington: A Picture Book Biography*. New York: Scholastic, 1992.

Hakim, Joy. *A History of US: From Colonies to Country: 1710–1791*. New York: Oxford University Press, 1993, 1999.

Harness, Cheryl. *George Washington*. Washington, D.C.: National Geographic Society, 2000.

Isaacs, Sally Senzell. *America in the Time of George Washington*. Des Plaines, Ill.: Heinemann Library, 1998.

Kent, Zachary. *Encyclopedia of Presidents: George Washington*. Chicago: Children's Press, 1986.

Mello, Tara Baukus. *George Washington: First U.S. President*. Philadelphia: Chelsea House Publishers, 1999.

Meltzer, Milton. *George Washington and the Birth of Our Nation*. New York: Franklin Watts, 1986.

Old, Wendie C. *United States Presidents: George Washington*. Springfield, N.J.: Enslow Publishers, 1997.

Osborne, Mary Pope. *George Washington: Leader of a New Nation*. New York: Dial Books for Young Readers, 1991.

Rosenburg, John. *Young George Washington*. Brookfield, Conn.: The Millbrook Press, 1997.

CHILDREN'S MAGAZINES

"Alexander Hamilton," *Cobblestone* 8, no. 3 (March 1987).

"Celebrating Our Constitution," *Cobblestone* 8, no. 9 (September 1987).

"Contest for Empire: 1754–1763," *Cobblestone* 12, no. 4 (April 1991).

"George Washington," *Cobblestone* 13, no. 4 (April 1992).

"Slavery at Mount Vernon," *Footsteps* 2, no. 5 (November/December 2000).

"Washington," *Kids Discover* 10, no. 8 (September 2000).

"The White House," *Cobblestone* 21, no. 6 (September 2000).

TEACHER MATERIALS

Hargrove, Julia. *George Washington's Farewell Address*. Carthage, Ill.: Teaching & Learning Company, 2000.

The Mount Vernon Ladies' Association. *George Washington: Gentleman from Mount Vernon*. Vol. 14, Teaching With Primary Sources Series. Peterborough, N.H.: Cobblestone Publishing, 1998.

BOOKS, PAMPHLETS, GUIDEBOOKS

Alden, John R. *George Washington: A Biography*. Baton Rouge: Louisiana State University Press, 1984.

Brookhiser, Richard. *Founding Father: Rediscovering George Washington*. New York: Free Press Paperbacks (Simon & Schuster), 1996.

Carrick, Elizabeth Bates. *The Rockingham Story*. Princeton, N.J.: The Rockingham Association, 1978.

Cunliffe, Marcus. *George Washington: Man and Monument*. New York: Mentor (Penguin Group), 1982.

Dutcher, David C. G. *Concise History of the American Revolution*. National Park American History Series, Eastern National, 1999.

Ferling, John E. *The First of Men: A Life of George Washington*. Knoxville: University of Tennessee Press, 1988.

Flexner, James Thomas. *Washington: The Indispensable Man*. Boston: Little, Brown & Company, 1974.

Freeman, Douglas Southall. *Washington*. New York: Touchstone (Simon & Schuster), 1995.

Grafton, John. *The American Revolution: A Picture Sourcebook*. New York: Dover Publications, 1975.

Independence National Historical Park. *Independence: A Guide to Independence National Historical Park*. Handbook 115. Washington, D.C.: Division of Publications, National Park Service, U.S. Department of the Interior, 1982.

Kaminski, John P., and Jill Adair McCaughan. *A Great and Good Man: George Washington in the Eyes of His Contemporaries*. Madison, Wis.: Madison House, 1989.

Ketchum, Richard M. *The World of George Washington*. New York: American Heritage Publishing Company, 1974.

Kinnaird, Clark. *George Washington: The Pictorial Biography*. New York: Hastings House, 1967.

Lerme, Deborah, and Diana Menkes. *George Washington, an American Icon: The Eighteenth-Century Graphic Portraits*. Based on the catalogue of the exhibition of the same title, written by Wendy C. Wick. Washington, D.C.: Smithsonian Institution Traveling Exhibition Service and the National Portrait Gallery, 1982.

Longmore, Paul K. *The Invention of George Washington*. Charlottesville: University Press of Virginia, 1999.

MacDonald, William. *George Washington: A Brief Biography*. Mount Vernon, Va.: The Mount Vernon Ladies' Association, 1987.

Mitnick, Barbara J. *The Changing Image of George Washington*. New York: Fraunces Tavern Museum, 1989.

———, ed. *George Washington: American Symbol*. New York: Hudson Hills Press, 1999.

Morgan, Edmund S. *The Genius of George Washington*. New York: W. W. Norton & Company, 1980.

Morristown National Historical Park. *Morristown: A History and Guide*. Handbook 120. Washington, D.C.: Division of Publications, National Park Service, U.S. Department of the Interior, 1983.

The Mount Vernon Ladies' Association. *Mount Vernon: A Handbook*. Mount Vernon, Va.: The Mount Vernon Ladies' Association of the Union, 1998.

Rhodehamel, John. *The Great Experiment: George Washington and the American Republic*. New Haven, Conn., and San Marino, Calif.: Yale University Press and The Huntington Library, 1998.

———. *George Washington: Writings*. New York: The Library of America, 1997.

The Seamen's Bank for Savings. *When George Washington Came to Wall Street*. New York: The Seamen's Bank for Savings in Cooperation with the New York City Commission on the Bicentennial of the Constitution, 1989.

Smith, Richard Norton. *Patriarch: George Washington and the New American Nation*. Boston: Houghton Mifflin Company, 1993.

ARTICLES

Abbot, W. W. "The Young George Washington and His Papers." Presented in the Dome Room of the University of Virginia Rotunda, 11 February 1999.

Billington, James H. "Letters from G. W." *Civilization*, February/March 1999.

Dunlap, David W. "Remodeled Tavern For a New Century." *New York Times*, Metro, 14 February 2001.

Ferling, John. "The Final Days." *American History*, December 1999.

Fleming, Thomas. "George Washington, Spymaster." *American Heritage*, February/March 2000.

Foote, Timothy. "Washington Slept Here." *Smithsonian*, December 1999.

Mastromarino, Mark. "Biography of George Washington." George Washington 1999 Bicentennial Site, The Mount Vernon Ladies' Association.

Redmond, Edward. "George Washington: Surveyor and Mapmaker." Library of Congress, Washington, D.C.
Available from memory.loc.gov/ammem/gmdhtml/gwmaps.html

Reif, Rita. "This Smile Warmed Martha's Heart." *New York Times*, 1 October 2000.

"Scholars on Washington." George Washington 1999 Bicentennial Site, The Mount Vernon Ladies' Association.

Schwartz, Stephan A. "George Mason: Forgotten Founder, He Conceived the Bill of Rights." *Smithsonian*, May 2000.

Smith, Richard Norton. "The Surprising George Washington." *Prologue: Quarterly of the National Archives and Records Administration*, Spring 1994.

Twohig, Dorothy. "George Washington: The First President." *Humanities*, January/February 1997.

———. "'That Species of Property': Washington's Role in the Controversy Over Slavery." in Don Higginbotham, ed., *George Washington Reconsidered* (Charlottesville, Va., University Press of Virginia, 2001), 114–138.

Ward, Geoffrey C. "Who Was Washington?" *American Heritage*, February/March 1993.

NONPRINT SOURCES

"The Crossing." Produced by Bob Christiansen and Rick Rosenberg and directed by Robert Harmon. 90 min., A&E Television Networks, 1999. Videocassette.

"Founding Fathers." History Channel, November 27, 2000. Television program.

"George Washington: Founding Father." Produced and directed by Adam Friedman and Monte Markham. 50 min. A&E Television Networks, 1999. Videocassette.

"George Washington—The Man Who Wouldn't Be King." Produced by David Sutherland. 60 min. PBS Video, 1992. Videocassette.

"George Washington: Music for the First President." Arnold, Md.: David and Ginger Hildebrand, 1999. Compact disc.

"The Life of George Washington." Produced by The Mount Vernon Ladies' Association. 30 min. MVLA/Finley-Holiday Film Corp., 1989. Videocassette.

Frederick MacMonnies's memorial in Princeton, New Jersey, celebrates the victory of Washington and his troops at the Battle of Princeton in early 1777.

PLACES TO VISIT: PARKS, MUSEUMS, LIBRARIES

MASSACHUSETTS

Museum of Fine Arts, Boston (www.mfa.org)

NEW JERSEY

The Historical Society of Princeton, Princeton (www.princetonhistory.org)

Morristown National Historical Park, Morristown (www.nps.gov/morr/index.htm)

Nassau Hall, Princeton

The New Jersey Historical Society, Newark (www.jerseyhistory.org)

Old Barracks Museum, Trenton (www.barracks.org)

Princeton Battlefield State Park and Thomas Clarke House, Princeton

The Princeton Battle Monument, Princeton

Princeton University Art Museum, Princeton (www.princetonartmuseum.org)

Rockingham State Historic Site, Franklin Township (www.rockingham.net)

Wallace House State Historic Site, Somerville

The sign at the Fraunces Tavern Museum features a portrait of George Washington.

NEW YORK

Federal Hall National Memorial, Manhattan (www.nps.gov/feha/index.htm)

Fraunces Tavern Museum, Manhattan (www.frauncestavernmuseum.org)

The Metropolitan Museum of Art, Manhattan (www.metmuseum.org)

St. Paul's Chapel, The Parish of Trinity Church, Manhattan (www.trinitywallstreet.org)

The huts of soldiers have been reconstructed at Valley Forge National Historical Park to allow visitors to understand what life was like there during the winter of 1777–78.

The statue outside Independence Hall pays tribute to George Washington.

PENNSYLVANIA

The David Library of the American Revolution, Washington Crossing (www.dlar.org)

Fort Necessity National Battlefield, Farmington (www.nps.gov/fone/index.htm)

Independence National Historical Park, Philadelphia (www.nps.gov/inde/index.htm)

Philadelphia Museum of Art, Philadelphia (www.philamuseum.org)

Valley Forge National Historical Park, Valley Forge (www.nps.gov/vafo/index.htm)

Washington Crossing Historic Park, Washington Crossing (www.phmc.state.pa.us/bhsm/toh/washington/washingtoncrossing.asp)

VIRGINIA

George Washington's Mount Vernon Estate and Gardens, Mount Vernon (www.mountvernon.org)

The Papers of George Washington, University of Virginia, Charlottesville (www.virginia.edu/gwpapers)

WASHINGTON, D.C.

George Washington Papers at the Library of Congress (http://memory.loc.gov/ammem/gwhtml/gwhome.html)

The Library of Congress (www.loc.gov)

TEXT AND PICTURE CREDITS

TEXT

Fitzpatrick, John, C., ed. *The Writings of George Washington from the Original Manuscript Sources: 1745–1799*. Washington, D.C.: United States Printing Office, 1931–1944: 46, 47–48, 49–51, 52–53, 54, 55–56, 57–58, 59, 61–62, 86, 87, 88–89, 89, 92

The following are reprinted with permission of the University Press of Virginia.

Jackson, Donald and Dorothy Twohig, eds. *The Diaries of George Washington*. Vols. 1 and 6. Charlottesville, Va.: University Press of Virginia, 1976 and 1979: 14, 16, 33, 118

COLONIAL SERIES

Colonial Series 1: 1748-August 1755: Abbot, W.W., ed. *The Papers of George Washington*. Charlottesville, Va.: University Press of Virginia, 1983: 15,18–19, 20, 21 (both), 23–24, 25–26

Colonial Series 4: November 1756-October 1757: Abbot, W.W., ed. *The Papers of George Washington*. Charlottesville, Va.: University Press of Virginia, 1984: 26–27

Colonial Series 6: September 1758-December 1760: Abbot, W.W., ed. *The Papers of George Washington*. Charlottesville, Va.: University Press of Virginia, 1988: 28, 29–30, 32

Colonial Series 8: June 1767-December 1771: Abbot, W.W. and Dorothy Twohig, eds. *The Papers of George Washington*. Charlottesville, Va.: University Press of Virginia, 1993: 34, 35–36

Colonial Series 9: January 1772-March 1774: Abbot, W.W. and Dorothy Twohig, eds. *The Papers of George Washington*. Charlottesville, Va.: University Press of Virginia, 1994: 36 (bottom)

REVOLUTIONARY WAR SERIES

Revolutionary War Series 1: June-September 1775: Chase, Philander D., ed. *The Papers of George Washington*. Charlottesville, Va.: University Press of Virginia, 1985: 38, 40–41, 41

Revolutionary War Series 5: June-August 1776: Chase, Philander D., ed. *The Papers of George Washington*. Charlottesville, Va.: University Press of Virginia, 1993: 43–44

Revolutionary War Series 6: August-October 1776: Chase, Philander D. and Frank E. Grizzard, Jr., eds. *The Papers of George Washington*. Charlottesville, Va.: University Press of Virginia, 1994: 44–45

CONFEDERATION SERIES

Confederation Series 1: January-July 1784: Abbot, W.W., ed. *The Papers of George Washington*. Charlottesville, Va.: University Press of Virginia, 1992: 63–64

Confederation Series 2: July 1784-May 1785: Abbot, W.W., ed. *The Papers of George Washington*. Charlottesville, Va.: University Press of Virginia, 1992: 64

Confederation Series 4: April 1786-January 1787: Abbot, W.W., ed. *The Papers of George Washington*. Charlottesville, Va.: University Press of Virginia, 1995: 66, 67

Confederation Series 5: February-December 1787: Abbot, W.W., ed. *The Papers of George Washington*. Charlottesville, Va.: University Press of Virginia, 1997: 69, 71, 72 (top)

Confederation Series 6: January-September 1788: Abbot, W.W., ed. *The Papers of George Washington*. Charlottesville, Va.: University Press of Virginia, 1997: 72 (bottom), 74

PRESIDENTIAL SERIES

Presidential Series 1: September 1788-March 1789: Twohig, Dorothy, ed. *The Papers of George Washington*. Charlottesville, Va.: University Press of Virginia, 1987: 75–76

Presidential Series 2: April-June 1789: Twohig, Dorothy, ed. *The Papers of George Washington*. Charlottesville, Va.: University Press of Virginia, 1987: 78, 80

Presidential Series 4: September 1789-January 1790: Twohig, Dorothy, ed. *The Papers of George Washington*. Charlottesville, Va.: University Press of Virginia, 1993: 82, 82-85

RETIREMENT SERIES

Retirement Series 1: March-December 1797: Abbot, W.W., ed. *The Papers of George Washington*. Charlottesville, Va.: University Press of Virginia, 1998: 112 (both)

Retirement Series 2: January-September 1798: Abbot, W.W., ed. *The Papers of George Washington*. Charlottesville, Va.: University Press of Virginia, 1998: 113–114

Retirement Series 4: April-December 1799: Abbot, W.W., ed. *The Papers of George Washington*. Charlottesville, Va.: University Press of Virginia, 1999: 116–117

The Papers of George Washington Web Site (www.virginia.edu/gwpapers): 91, 94–110

PICTURE

Carolyn P. Yoder: 134 (top)

Carolyn P. Yoder. Courtesy of Sons of the Revolution in the State of New York, Inc./Fraunces Tavern® Museum, New York City: 133 (bottom)

FTM ACC NO: 1985.2.1. Sons of the Revolution in the State of New York, Inc./Fraunces Tavern® Museum, New York City: 62

FTM ACC NO: 1965.2.1. Sons of the Revolution in the State of New York, Inc./Fraunces Tavern® Museum, New York City: 70 (bottom)

FTM ACC NO: 1936.2.24. Sons of the Revolution in the State of New York, Inc./Fraunces Tavern® Museum, New York City: 33

FTM ACC NO: 1936.2.5. Sons of the Revolution in the State of New York, Inc./Fraunces Tavern® Museum, New York City: 77 (bottom)

Grafton, Carol Belanger, editor, *Old-Fashioned Patriotic Cuts*. Mineola, N.Y.: Dover Publications, Inc., 1988: 122 (all), 124 (bottom), 125 (bottom)

Grafton, John. *The American Revolution: A Picture Sourcebook*. Mineola, N.Y.: Dover Publications, Inc., 1975: 42, 46, 48, 54, 117, 121, 123 (all), 124 (top), 125 (top), 126

Independence National Historical Park: 65, 70 (top), 81, 94, 112

K. A. Mason: background cover, 60 (all), 68 (all), 133 (top), 134 (bottom)

Courtesy of the Library of Congress, Prints and Photographs Division: LC-USZ62-112547: 9; LC-USZ62-113387: 31; LC-USZ62-3912:73; LC-USZ62-114284: 77 (top); LC-USZ62-110721:79; LC-USZ62-091986: 89; LC-USZ62-117747: 90; LC-USZ62-103188: 119 (top)

From the Collections of The New Jersey Historical Society: 115, 119 (bottom)

From the Collections of The New York Public Library, Astor, Lenox, and Tilden Foundations: 6

North Wind Picture Archives: 13, 17 (all), 22, 25, 32, 39, 41, 111, 128

Courtesy of the Pennsylvania Academy of the Fine Arts, Philadelphia. Bequest of William Bingham: 93

Courtesy of the Pennsylvania Academy of the Fine Arts, Philadelphia. Gift of Maria McKean Allen and Phebe Warren Downes through the bequest of their mother, Elizabeth Wharton McKean: 3

This portrait currently hangs in Tanglewood, the residence of the President of West Chester University of Pennsylvania: 50

U.S. Department of the Interior, National Park Service, Saint-Gaudens National Historic Site, Cornish, N.H.: 129, 137

INDEX

In 1889, sculptor Augustus Saint-Gaudens created this bronze medal for the hundredth-year anniversary of Washington's inauguration as the country's first president.

Note: The initials GW and MW in the index stand for George and Martha Washington, respectively.